Student Projects

- Ideas and Plans

Author and Editor:

Lois Roets Ed.D.

The ink drawing on the cover is the creation of a high school student:

Peggy Chamra

Peg is pictured by her current painting project - a ballet dancer.

STUDENT PROJECTS - IDEAS & PLANS, © 1994, Leadership Publishers

Leadership Publishers Inc.
Promoting Leadership & Human Potential
Post Office Box 8358
Des Moines, Iowa 50301-8358

Student Projects - Ideas & Plans
1994 edition
ISBN: 0 - 911943 - 39 -0

Student Projects - Ideas and Plans

Table of Contents

√ *Italics = new to this edition*

"I am a 3/4 combination classroom teacher. I found STUDENT PROJECTS - IDEAS & PLANS to be very helpful to those students who liked to do special projects and activities in my regular classroom. The book gave students lots of ideas for projects they could work on. Everyone was most anxious to look through the book and find something they wanted to do. The enthusiasm caught on. The book was a great aid for me." *Marilyn Kruse   Des Moines, Iowa*

"Lois Roets has been a presenter at summer Confratutes held at the University of Connecticut at Storrs. Her programs and manners of presentation were well-received by participants at the Confratute. The programs she writes are suitable for Type 1 - introductory activity, Type II - skills training sessions. Each program provides endless opportunities for Type III - independent student projects." *Dr. Joe Renzulli, University of Connecticut*

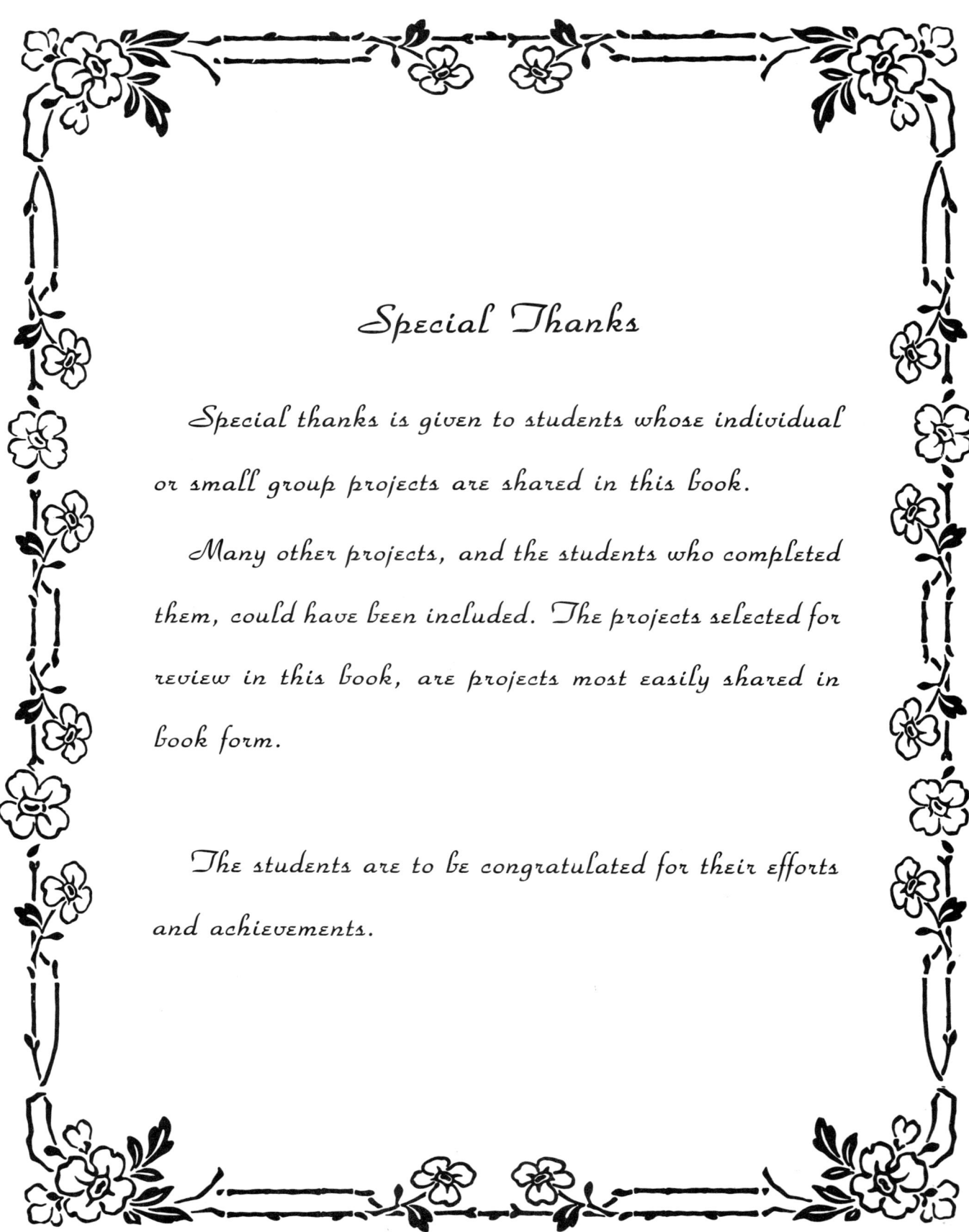

Special Thanks

Special thanks is given to students whose individual or small group projects are shared in this book.

Many other projects, and the students who completed them, could have been included. The projects selected for review in this book, are projects most easily shared in book form.

The students are to be congratulated for their efforts and achievements.

PURPOSE OF BOOK

The purpose of this book is fourfold:

To provide project ideas to students.

To share some completed student projects with readers of this book.

To encourage teachers to provide opportunities for individual or small group student projects.

To provide forms for planning individual or small group projects.

THE VALUE OF STUDENT PROJECTS

Teachers are urged to encourage students to plan individual or small group projects. Individual student projects, or small group projects, are <u>the</u> way to:

1. match assignments to student rate of learning,

2. increase knowledge level in a particular subject,

3. learn to put a plan/idea into action,

4. learn more skills at a time when a student is highly motivated to learn new skills.

5. provide for individual differences within any standard class curriculum,

6. provide the opportunity to pursue a topic of interest,

7. provide opportunity to increase self-awareness of abilities as learned through working on an individual project, and

8. provide opportunity for peer support through group review of completed projects.

Student Projects - Ideas & Plans. © Leadership Publishers,1994

Two Basic Ways to Modify Standard Curriculum to Meet the Needs of High-Ability Learners

There are two basic ways in which standard curriculum should be modified to meet the needs of high-ability learners:

1. Ask open-ended questions that require comparison, synthesis, insight, judgment, hypothesis, conjecture, assimilation, personal opinion - and all other higher-order thinking and problem-solving skills you know or can develop.

2. Modify (differentiate) some assignments and classtime participation to provide time to pursue an alternate assignment or an independent study project.

Student Flexibility

Students should be permitted to skip needless drill and repetition so that they can pursue independent study. This flexibility ensures that students will not be held back by the standard curriculum. Through independent study, high-ability highly-motivated students will have the encouragement, time, and opportunity to improve their skills and increase knowledge. As for the other students, you may be surprised at what they will do if given the opportunity to work on an independent student project!

Independent student projects permit a wide range of student initiative and participation. Because students take responsibility for the projects, motivation is increased. Independent projects also permit minimum to maximum research, organization, reporting skills.

Portfolio/Authentic Assessment & Student Projects

Independent projects may become part of a student's portfolio. *A portfolio is a collection of completed works or works-in-progress which represent student efforts.* These "efforts" include but are not limited to: best work, skill mastered, insight gained, technique developed, reason for abandoning one problem-solving technique for another, and any other knowledge, skill, insight, pursuit that is important to the student. The portfolio, along with traditional measures of ability and achievement, then becomes authentic assessment.

This book is for teacher, student or parent use. Enjoy!

How do Independent Student Projects Fit into the Standard Curriculum?

Every standard curriculum content area has the opportunity for independent student projects. The project may flow directly from the regular curriculum or from student interest. Students will have their own ideas. Or, hand this book to them and say "Look through this book for ideas."

The independent project is the opportunity for the student to go into greater depth or to pursue a special interest. Students will also learn many skills as they plan, organize and complete a project.

Completed student projects should be reviewed with appropriate audiences. In this process, other students will learn and the student completing the project receives suggestions and encouragement.

Time to Work

The time to work on projects comes from regular classroom time. Drill and repetition should be eliminated when the student already has demonstrated mastery of the content. At other times, simpler assignments should be skipped so that students have time to pursue independent projects. Students negotiate - "buy time"- for projects related to their interests and talent.

Grading Independent Projects

How do you grade independent projects? The answers are:
√ carefully, √ not at all, √ "for comments only",
√ extra credit, √ self-rating,
√ any other system agreeable to the teacher and student.
Whatever system is used, the students should know how the project will be evaluated before beginning the project.

Sharing Independent Projects

In an effort to encourage high achievement and motivation to learn, some schools host a yearly/semester "Student Projects Fair." All student projects are exhibited in one location. Parents, relatives, community members, as well as other students, may visit the exhibits.

Exhibiting students will feel pride in sharing their work. They will also see the works of other students. More students are then inspired to pursue an independent project. The total school and community will be proud of efforts and achievements earned through individual and small group projects.

Relationship between Student Projects and Talent Awareness & Development

Individual/small group student projects help students become aware of talent, interests. They also provide opportunity to develop and share that talent.

Talent is a real ability residing within an individual. It comes from one or more of these factors:
- ❐ genetic inheritance,
- ❐ environment, or
- ❐ chance-"luck of the draw".

Talent is recognized and confirmed by a quick grasp of the content/skill of the talent.

Examples:
- √ *learns with few (1-3) or no repetitions,*
- √ *anticipates the next level of performance, asks all the right questions,*
- √ *sees far-reaching implication or application to the material learned,*
- √ *masters subject matter / skill quickly after initial orientation.*

There is also intense interest in the subject. "Intense interest" is defined as:
- ◆ maintaining focused attention,
- ◆ sustaining interest for a long time,
- ◆ assigning high priority to the topic in terms of time and resources,
- ◆ searching for or accepting additional opportunities.

Once talent is recognized, it has to be valued by the society in which it exists and is expressed. Talent that has no chance to be recognized or expressed will not develop. Unrecognized or undeveloped talent is a loss to society and a frustration to the person who yearns to use it. The person is frustrated because there is "something inside" that is pushing to get out but few opportunities or rewards for letting the talent develop.

Talent develops when there are opportunities to:
- • practice the talent,
- • perform/share the talent with/for others,
- • receive feedback on talent expression,
- • perfect it.

Student Projects and Individual Differences

Learning/behavioral Styles

All high-ability and gifted & talented students may not learn in the same way. There is a wide range of interests, behavioral and learning styles. There are two predominant learning/behavioral types of students: 1. Movers & Shakers 2. Receivers.

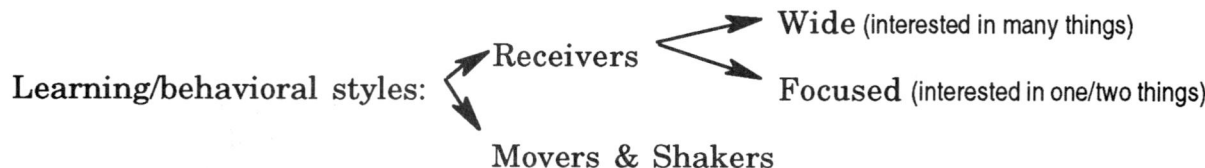

Learning/behavioral styles:
Receivers
Wide (interested in many things)
Focused (interested in one/two things)
Movers & Shakers

The Movers & Shakers

<u>Observable behaviors:</u>

-They create and challenge systems.
-They like to know what is expected of them - the end
   product - but seldom want nor need explicit
   directions on how to complete the product.
-They often have many projects going on at the same time
   - a few of which will succeed and the rest are rejected.
-Trial-and-error is the preferred method of problem-solving.
-Their desks tend to be messy because of all the things going
   on at the same time. This "messiness" permits the
   student to see various stimuli at once or continuously.
   For them, this helps the creativity/production process.
-While their minds are always working (we can't see this), their
   productivity (we can see this) appears to come in "spurts".

<u>You will frustrate the Movers & Shakers by</u>
√ giving too **many** directives,
√ being unclear about the end product,
√ providing too little time to think about/complete the solution,
√ being inflexible on minor details,
√ interrupting their work time or changing directions too many times,
√ forcing them to work in groups - all the time (you cannot
   expect a group of people to continuously and collectively create
   -- Michelangelo, Beethoven, Einstein created individually)
√ being insensitive to the strong emotions these students often have,
√ always expecting paper & pencil, research papers and reports.
   They prefer a variety/change: seminars, field trips, interviews, plays....

Student Projects - Ideas & Plans. © Leadership Publishers,1994

The Receivers
Observable behaviors:
-They function best when explicit guidelines for sequence
of curriculum and assignments are given. Explicit
directions are given for what to study, what to skip,
and what is the next step to take.
-They like to work at one thing at a time,
-They are focused to the task at hand,
-They tend to be neat and orderly,
-They can concentrate on one subject for a long time,
-They are often our best candidates for acceleration.
-They are comfortable competing against themselves or others.

Receivers can be of two types:
Wide Receivers - who "soak up" all the learning experiences you
can provide in as many content areas as possible.
Focused Receivers - who have a particular area of interest and
will take every opportunity to pursue that interest
through additional study, field trip, research project,
interviews and attendance at seminars.

You will frustrate Receivers by:
√ giving too **few** directives,
√ being unclear about the end product,
√ providing too little instruction on how to achieve the desired learning,
√ being unclear about the details and timeline,
√ interrupting their work time or changing directions,
√ forcing them to work with Movers & Shakers too much of the time.
While "trial & error and lots of activity" is the style of Movers & Shakers,
"Slow-and-steady-wins-the-race/One-thing-at-a-time" is the Receivers'
style. The Receivers' plea is this: "Tell me what to do and I'll do it."
√ assuming high-ability learners always know what to do,
√ making them create manipulatives: posters, plays,.... They like
pencil & paper, research, reports.

Competition and Motivation:

All high ability students are competitive but the source of competition may not be the same. There are those who complete with self and those who compete with others.

Competitive styles: < Compete-with-self (compete with their own record)

Compete-with-others (use high records of others to set the rate of achievement)

The compete-with-self elects to compete with their own personal level of achievement: to maintain their top score, to improve their top score, to do better on one particular category.... The compete-with-others looks at the achievment of others to define the competition. They set their goal to surpass the current "top".

Competition and motivation are closely related. The "self-competitor" is motivated by her own internal sense of control and the external reinforcements that come from it. The "compete-with-others" is motivated by knowing the highest achievement of others and then trying to do better than that level. They use others to help set achievement levels.

Caution

In no ways are these categories of behavior, learning or motivation meant to be exclusive or stereotypical. A person may be one type in one situation and may respond differently in another situation or environment. Use the information presented here to help you work with many types of students in many different situations.

Portfolio/Authentic Assessment & Student Projects

Independent projects may become part of a student's portfolio. *A portfolio is a collection of completed works or works-in-progress which represent student efforts.* These "efforts" include but are not limited to: best work, skill mastered, insight gained, technique developed, reason for abandoning one problem-solving technique for another, and any other knowledge, skill, insight, pursuit that is important to the student. The portfolio, along with traditional measures of ability and achievement, then becomes authentic assessment.

This book is for teacher, student or parent use. Enjoy!

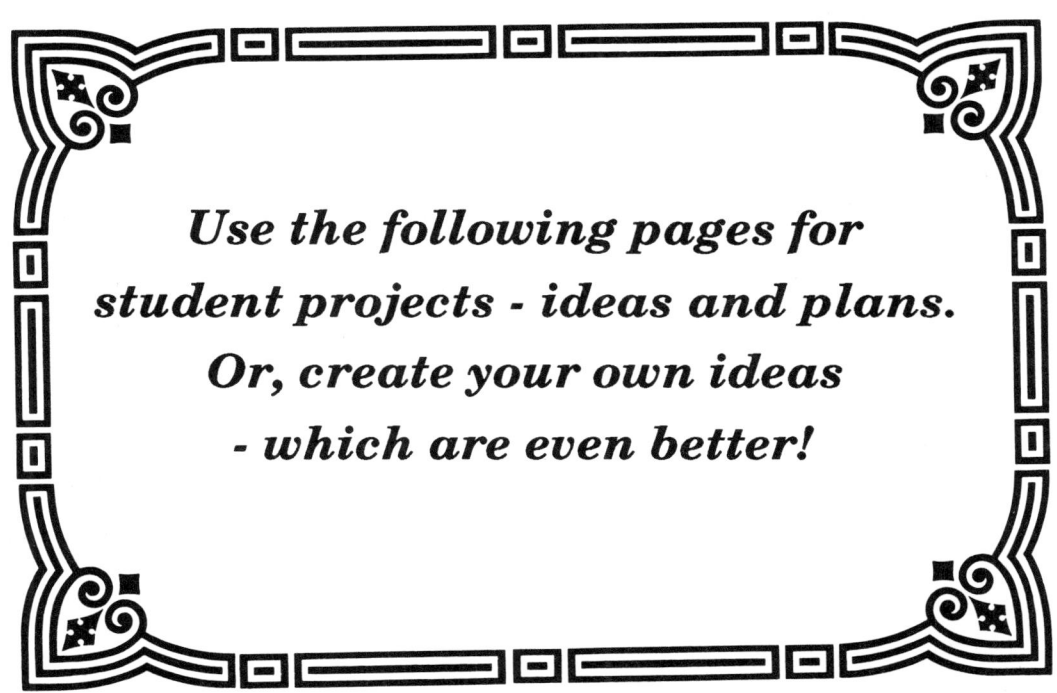

Use the following pages for student projects - ideas and plans. Or, create your own ideas - which are even better!

Artists

1. Read about artists.

2. Study the works of one artist.

3. Visit an art museum.

4. Visit an art gallery.

5. Make a matching quiz - matching artist with art creation.

6. List art pictures which are sometimes incorporated into ads or commercials.

   Example: American Gothic by Grant Wood
   Mona Lisa by Leonardo da Vinci

7. Study art works from a particular period or type of art. *Example:* Impressionism

PICASSO

Manet

Goya

Monet

Renoir

Degas

Rembrandt

Van Gogh

Turner

Homer

CASSATT

Write a fictional story . . .

about   anything

you   would

like

to write

about

(These pictures may give <u>some</u> ideas!)

Collect . . .

leaves

dolls

photographs

rocks

stuffed animals

buttons

books

music: tapes, records & CD's

spoons

jokes

baseball cards

autographs

model: cars, trains, airplanes ....

seashells

souvenirs: elephants, cats, bells ....

calendars

ribbons & bows

memorabilia: Civil War, centennials, ...

masks

coins

stamps

concert tickets

feathers

pencils or pens

pennants

napkins from special occasions

autographed pictures of famous people

regional Stories: folklore, home cures ....

Ancestors & Kin

NEWS

Today's
information.

&

REPORTS

Information from books and other sources.

&

TALES

Fictitious accounts
and folktales.

Three poems by Lisa Brown, *Spencer, Iowa.*

Spring

Spring, Spring where have you been?
    Winter left then came back again.
Summer, Summer there **you** are!
    Now where's spring?
Well, now Fall is coming near;
    But **I'm** waiting for Spring to get here.
Spring, Spring where are you? I guess I've
just lost you.

Haiku

Blossoming, blooming
Ev'rything's pretty in Spring
Pretty as a rose.

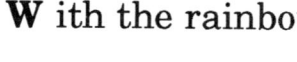

Rainbows

R ainbows are beautiful

A s beautiful as they can be

I n the rain sometimes I see rainbows

N ot that I watch for rainbows all the time

B ut when I do see rainbows I can see Angels in them

O ut in the Heavens way up there

W ith the rainbows

S inging songs of praise to God.

Write a poem . . .

Poetry expresses:

love

amusing thoughts

ideas

feelings

speculations

fear

grandeur of the moment

loyalty

history

hope

Travel

Make a booklet of . . .

— *stories*

— *plays*

— *photographs*

— *quotations*

— *recipes*

— *fashions*

— *art pictures*

— *fabric samples*

— *friends*

— *pets*

— *happy memories*

— *ideas*

— *jokes*

— *riddles*

— *unusual words*

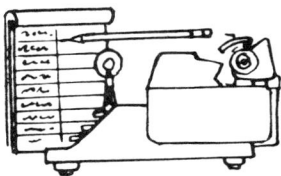

INFORMATION BOX

Science Fiction stories change some facts or suggest a world/people different from what we know and understand.

Science Fiction will often:
   a. change the environment and keep people, plants and animals as we know them,
                          or
   b. change people, plants or animals and keep the environment as we understand it.

RECOMMENDATION: Do not change both the environment and people/plants/animals. The reader may become too confused to read and understand and enjoy your story.

Write science fiction . . .

Changes in people or animals or plants:

Changes in the environment:

Student Projects - Ideas & Plans. © Leadership Publishers, 1994

INFORMATION BOX

Science Fiction creates a world that could have been

or may someday be.

1. Write a science fiction story in which the <u>environment</u> stays the same as it is today. But, the <u>creatures</u> who live in this environment are different from creatures we know.

2. Write a science fiction story in which the <u>people</u> are the same as you and me. But, the <u>environment</u> is different.
   (Examples of environmental changes: no oxygen,
   plants walk . . .

3. Read science fiction. If this is a new area of reading, start with Isaac Asimov or Ray Bradbury. <u>Science fiction</u> is the literary genre that has gained much popularity over the last 40 years.

4. Adapt a science fiction book into a play to be acted on stage, or read in reader's theatre production.

5. Impersonate a character from a science fiction book.

6. Write a letter to a science fiction writer. Send the letter in care of the publishing house that published the author's book(s).

7. Take one fact of science and turn it into science fiction — that is, change "fact" in some way to make it "fiction."

8. Read as many science fiction stories as you can. Keep a list of readings.

HEAT

1. *List ways to survive during very hot seasons. Make this specific to your geographic area.*

2. *List dangers associated with intense heat.*

3. *Collect answers to "It was so hot ...."*

4. *Collect stories of real-life adventures and events associated with hot weather.*

5. *Read books that tell about hot places and/or adventures that took place under intense heat conditions.*

1. COLLECT STORIES OF REAL-LIFE EVENTS THAT TOOK PLACE DURING COLD WEATHER.

2. LIST WAYS TO STAY WARM. THIS SHOULD BE SPECIFIC TO YOUR GEOGRAPHIC AREA.

3. LIST DANGERS ASSOCIATED WITH THE COLD.

4. READ BOOKS THAT TELL ABOUT COLD WEATHER ADVENTURES.

5. COLLECT ANSWERS TO THIS : "It was so cold that..."

6. MEMORIZE FREEZING AND BOILING POINTS AS MEASURED ON DIFFERENT THERMOMETERS.

7. WHICH DOGS OR OTHER ANIMALS ARE ASSOCIATED WITH COLD AREAS?

Sports Cards for the Home Team

Student Project by: James D. White Bishop Garrigan High School Algona, Iowa

Faculty Advisors:
David M. Burrow, Gifted & Talented Program Coordinator
Steve Brosnan, Art Department Head

*Here are two cards from the 1992 set. The front and reverse side are
shown for the developer of this excellent project, James D. White,
and his friend, Torrey.*

Reverse Side	Reverse Side
10 height:6'1" weight:175 bats:right throws:right acquired:by GHS,'89 born:9/26/74 home:Algona,IA	**11** height:6'3" weight:195 bats:right throws:right acquired:by GHS,'90 born:5/19/75 home:Wesley,IA

JAMES D. WHITE * OF

Yr	Club	AB	R	H	RBI	2B	3B	HR	W	SO	SB	AVE
'91	GHS	62	14	37	41	11	2	1	9	7	9	.597

James's favorite baseball player is Don Mattingly.
Mr. White is the son of Evelyn.

TORREY M. WINGERT * 1B

Yr	Club	AB	R	H	RBI	2B	3B	HR	W	SO	SB	AVE
91	GHS	55	25	23	19	4	2	1	9	5	10	.418

Torrey is an exceptional athlete,he made first team
All-State in basketball.His teammates call him "Bill".
Mr. Wingert is the son of Stephen and Marla.

**Read the next two pages describing how this project was done.
James also listed eight "Hints". Thanks, James!** ☞

"How to" for <u>*Sports Cards for the Home Team*</u> - *James D. White*

Project: **Design and market sports cards for a sports team from your local high school**

Necessary Steps:

1. Check into printing possibilities (black & white/color; quality of card stock, 1 or 2 sides, size....) their costs, time requirements, and exactly what you need to give the printer. Do "comparison pricing" among local printers and mail order services.

2. Make arrangements for financing the project. Costs will range from $100 (for a small run of black & white cards) to $1000 (for a large run of color cards). Sources of funding include booster clubs, parent groups, or student councils - which could sell the cards as a fundraiser.)

3. Make a timetable of what needs to be done when.

4. Decide which players to include (all players, stars, starters,....). The number you choose will affect the size of sheets and the cost of printing.

5. Acquire good quality photos of the players. Take them yourself, or get them from the yearbook files or your local newspaper. Make sure you give the printers what they need - black & white prints, color slides, negatives, halftones, ... You may need to do at least some of the photographic processing yourself.

6. Compile accurate statistics on the players.

7. Come up with a standard design for both the fronts and backs of the cards. Computer design programs are helpful here.

8. Individually design the fronts and backs of each cards. Proofread and double-check everything.

9. Take the completed designs to the printer.

10. Package and arrange the printed cards for selling. Have some uncut sheets and team sets available, because parents and players will pay extra for them as souvenirs.

"How to" for <u>Sports Cards for the Home Team</u> - *James D. White*

Hints:

--- Know what your getting into. This is a tough project that involves organizing a lot of different things all at once. You'll get a crash course in how the business world works, and on top of that you'll learn about art, photography, computers, math, and whatever sport you choose.

--- If you do this project for more than one year in a row, it's <u>a lot</u> easier the second time around.

--- Color printing costs <u>much</u> more than black & white and it's probably not worth the cost. Remember that you have to sell a lot more color cards to return your up-front investment. Another cheap option is two-color printing, maybe in your school colors.

--- You'll probably do better with a local printer to whom you can talk personally and often. You'll get exactly what you want -- even if it costs a little bit more.

--- Plan on having leftover cards, and print more than you think you'll need. Little kids will want single cards of your school's stars, so you'll have a lot of leftovers from the players who sit on the bench all year. Be sure to set your prices with this in mind.

--- Advertising helps sales. Make sure you get the word out that the cards are available, and where people can buy them. Tell everyone you know and have the players tell everyone they know. Make posters and have the announcer at games advertise your cards. You might get the local paper or radio station to do a feature about it.

--- Get your financial arrangements taken care of <u>FIRST</u> -- before you commit to anything. This is a risky project. If you use your own money and things go wrong, you could lost a bundle. (I made about $500 on black & white cards the first year, which I split with a school group that was backing me. The second year I went on my own, and I lost a lot of money on expensive color cards.)

--- Arrange with the coach to have an "autograph session" after a big game. All the little kids will come to the game and buy cards, so they can meet their high school heroes. It also makes all the players feel really important. CAUTION: Make sure you pick a game you know you're going to win. No one's going to want to stick around for autographs after a loss.

--- Enjoy the project and learn all you can.

Athletic NEWS

Today's information.

& REPORTS

Information from books and other sources.

& TALES

Fictitious accounts and folktales.

Project **choices**

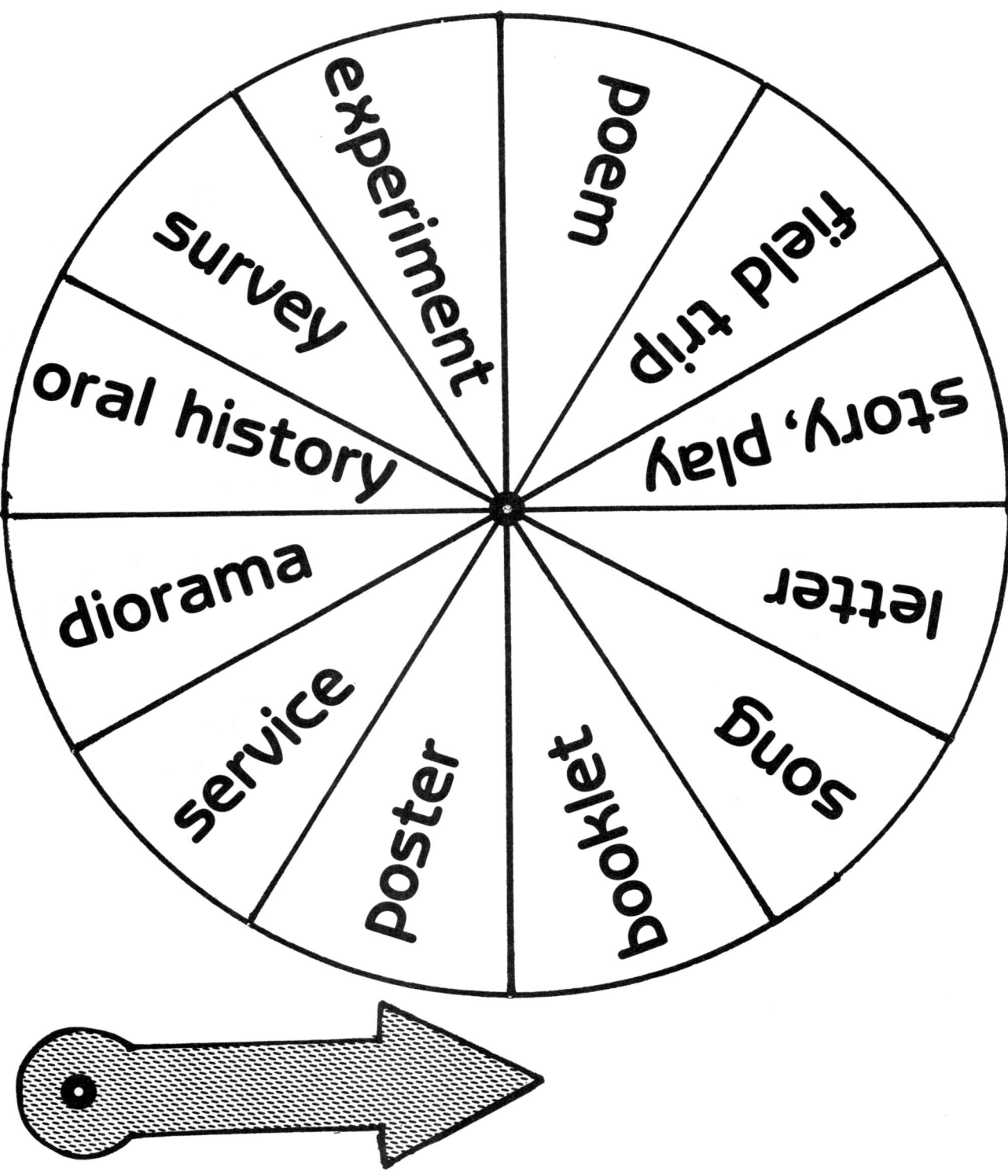

Action choices

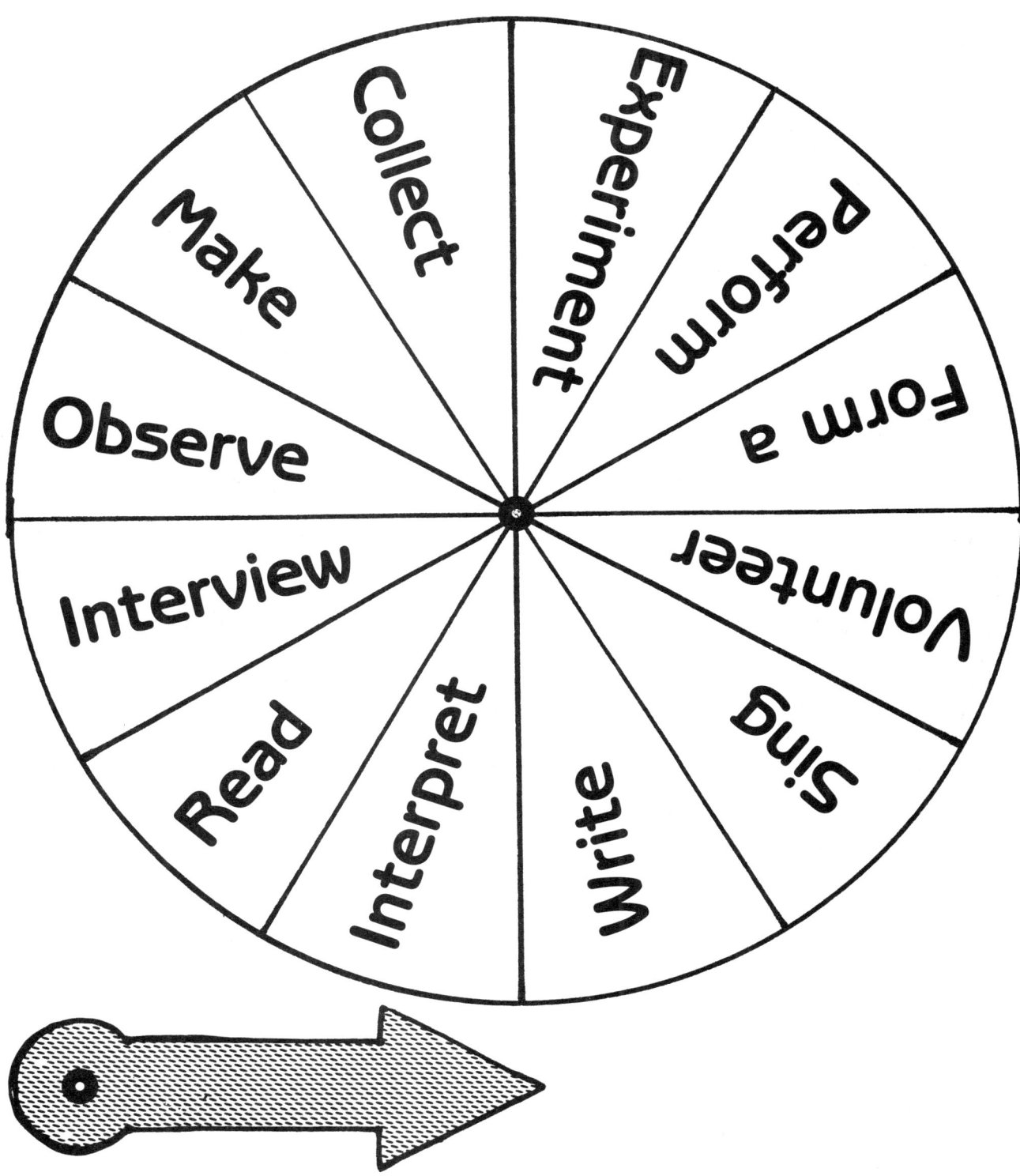

snow

Project: poem   story   song   poster   slide presentation

Topic Ideas:

S
n
o
w

Beauty of snow...

Living in snowy regions...

The value of snow to the economy...

The contents of snow...

Recreational activities related to snow...

The danger of snow...

Terms related to snow (snowdrift)...

Lifestyle of those who live in
snow regions...

How snow is formed...

A LIBRARY.

A MUSEUM.

    READ TO SOMEONE WHO IS ILL.

    TAKE CARE OF A CHILD OR CHILDREN.

    HELP IN FUND-RAISING FOR A NONPROFIT ORGANIZATION.

A HOSPITAL.

A SCHOOL.

    AN ELDERLY NEIGHBOR OR FRIEND.

    WRITE A LETTER FOR SOMEONE WHO CANNOT WRITE.

BOOKS

Education **Classics**

Read about . . .
Classify . . .
Write a report on . . .
Interview someone who . .
Compare one . . . to . . .
Hypothesize about . . .
Make a diorama of . . .

Write a play . . .
Perform a play . . .
Write a song . . .

Make a booklet of . . .
Draw a picture . . .
Collect . . .

Do a survey to find out . . .
Volunteer your services to . . .

Read poetry . . .
Write a poem . . .
Assemble a bibliography . . .
Write science fiction . . .
Write a fictional story . . .
Make a poster of . . .
Interpret . . .
Translate . . .
. . . other . . .

Student Projects - Ideas & Plans. © Leadership Publishers, 1994

Women
of
Achievement

1. Who are they?

2. What did each achieve?

3. Make a crossword puzzle or
   or word search on
   women of achievement.

4. Make a poster.

5. Read a biography of a
   famous person.

Write a play. . .

Perform a play. . .

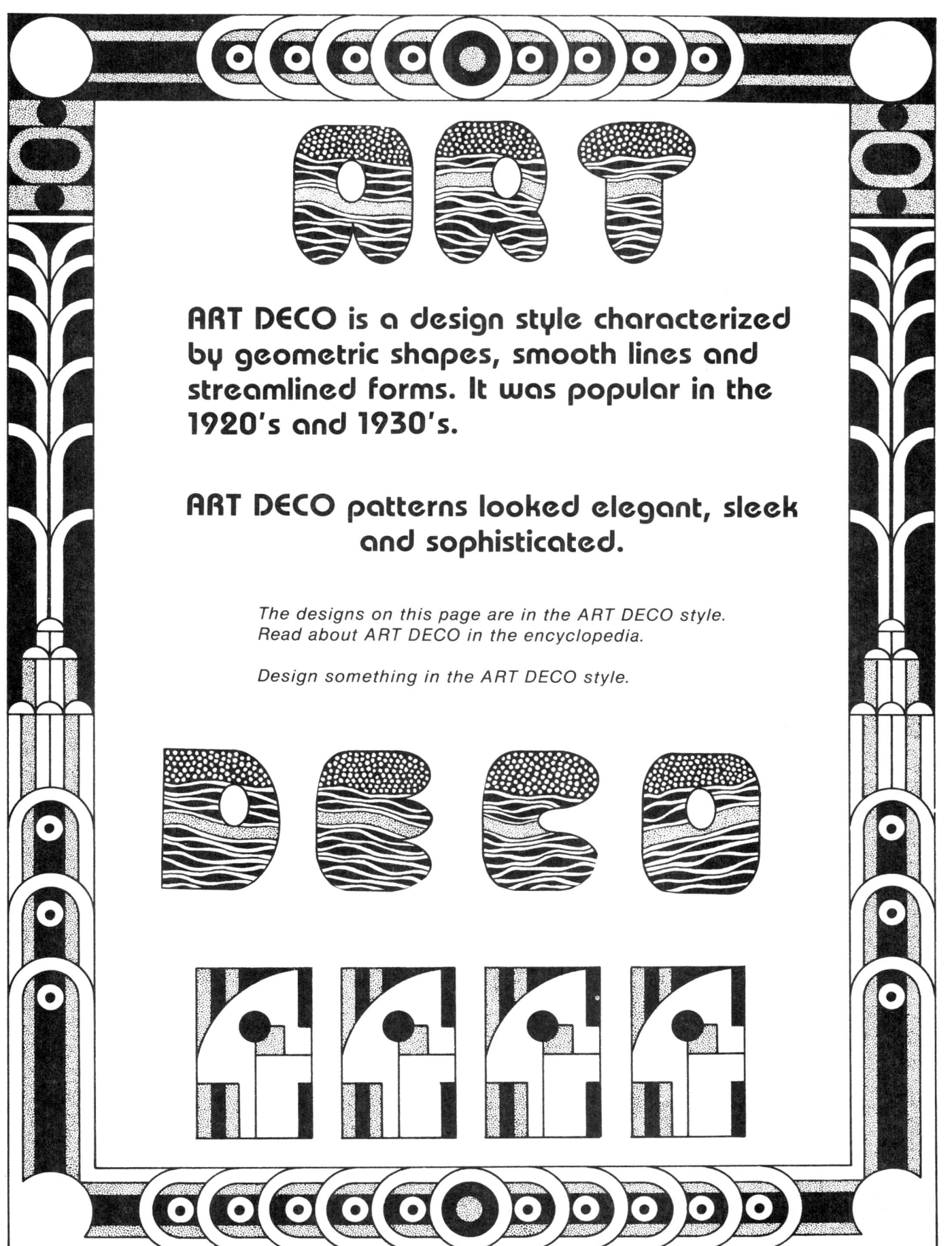

ART

ART DECO is a design style characterized by geometric shapes, smooth lines and streamlined forms. It was popular in the 1920's and 1930's.

ART DECO patterns looked elegant, sleek and sophisticated.

The designs on this page are in the ART DECO style. Read about ART DECO in the encyclopedia.

Design something in the ART DECO style.

DECO

Cartoons and Caricatures

Student Project

Student: **MICHAEL FRY**, *sophomore,* has enjoyed drawing cartoon characters. Here are two of **MIKE**'s athletic cartoons and caricatures.

Michael Fry

Student Projects - Ideas & Plans. © Leadership Publishers, 1994

Draw ^*paint* a picture...

CARTOONS

1. Read about "Cartooning" in a book.

2. There are five general types of cartoons. Read about each: 1) editorial or political, 2) comic strips , 3) gag, 4) illustrative (used to explain stories or advertisements), and 5) animated.

3. Draw a face. Make many sketches of that face. Make each sketch show a different emotion: fear, sadness, happiness, dizziness, craftiness.

4. Read about cartoonists who have shaped the world of entertainment. These could be the cartoonists who created Mickey Mouse, Garfield, Snoopy and other well-known characters.

5. Use the daily or Sunday newspaper most frequently read in your area. Survey students to see which cartoons are read regularly. Repeat the survey with adults.

6. Speculate: "Why are cartoons funny?"

7. From the daily paper, collect one week's political cartoons. Explain the message of each cartoon.

8. Using one topic of current political significance, draw a political cartoon giving your opinion of the issue.

Binary Numeration System

Jennifer Trier, Matt O'Gara, Jeff Siasoco, Kate Fletcher
Des Moines, Iowa

These students challenged themselves to learn the Binary Numeration System. They did so to master a computer program that included 10 categories of number problems - one of which was converting a number in one base system into the base two system. Base two uses only two digits: 0,1.

Example:
10 base ten = 1010 base two

What new information can you learn about numbers and numeration systems?

Arithmetic   Numbers

Mathematics

1. Read the history of mathematics.

       2. Make a dictionary of mathematical symbols.

3. Do a report on Euclid or other mathematician.

       4. Work number puzzles.

5. Design number puzzles.

       6. Describe a base ten number notation. Write that same numerical value in another base system.

7. Interview people to see if they like to do number problems and/or number puzzles.

       8. Use numbers and mathematical terms to compose a song or write a poem.

9. List 20 times during the day that numbers and mathematical concepts are used.
       Examples: *telling time*
                cooking a recipe
                running a race

       10. Write a set of nursey rhymes or poems that will help young children learn to count to "10".

FARM

NEWS

Today's information.

&

&

TALES

*Fictitious accounts
and folktales.*

REPORTS

Information from books and other sources.

Farming and Agriculture

1. Read the "Agriculture" section in an encyclopedia.

2. Write a report on the history of agriculture.

3. Make a products map of your continent. Show which kinds of agriculture are prevalent in each section.

4. Discuss: *"The development of agriculture is directly related to the rise in the standard of living."*

5. Make a timeline that shows inventions which improved agricultural methods and procedures.

6. Make a collage which shows agriculture through the ages.

7. Make a collage which shows agriculture as practiced in your geographic area.

8. Write a report about farming in your area.

9. Interview a farmer. Ask questions about the equipment used, busiest times of the year, and related questions.

THIS IS A CORNPICKER.

10. Visit a food processing or canning company. Learn and see how large quantities of food are cleaned, processed and shipped.

WIND

1. What is it?

2. How is it formed?

3. Describe it:

   beauty...

   power...

   danger...

   advantage...

   disadvantage...

   softness..

   movements.

Read about . . .
Classify . . .
Write a report on . . .
Interview someone who . . .
Compare one . . . to . . .
Hypothesize about . . .
Make a diorama of . . .
Take a field trip to . . .
Use a computer to . . .
Make a poster of . . .
Invent a . . .
Do a survey to find out . . .
Volunteer your services to . . .
Write a play . . .

Perform a play . . .
Write a song . . .
Sing a solo . . .
Form a musical group . . .
Collect oral history about . . .
Make a booklet of . . .
Draw a picture . . .
Collect . . .
Read poetry . . .
Write a poem . . .
Assemble a bibliography . . .
Write science fiction . . .
Write a fictional story . . .
Observe . . .
Experiment . . .

TREES

trees

Student Projects - Ideas & Plans. © Leadership Publishers, 1994

Historical Moments

1. Describe the importance of one historical moment.

2. Visit a museum that specializes in a particular historic emphasis.

3. Write a play explaining the historical moment and the importance thereof.

4. Take slides. Arrange a slide presentation on a historical moment.

5. As you see it, who are the "heroes" of history?

6. Collect oral history from someone whose life experiences differ from your own experiences.

7. In your local community, list 3 or more historical moments considered to be significant to the community.

8. Take one historic moment and consider the results if the outcome had been different.

   Examples: If the south had won the Civil War

   If George Washington had refused to lead the American Colonists.

   If Canada had joined the Colonists in the war for independence from England.

Persons Who Believed
in
Specific Causes

MARTIN LUTHER KING, Jr.

1. Who are they?

2. What means did they use to champion the cause?

3. How was the person reviewed in newspaper articles?

4. List persons and their causes currently in the news.

5. Why is it necessary that an individual be associated with a specific cause? (Discuss)

6. Make a chart covering a specific period of time, or the history of one country, listing the <u>cause</u>, the <u>person</u> fighting for it, and the <u>outcome</u> (if already resolved).

Give a Speech

Prepare and

1. about a particular place.

2. about something you saw yesterday.

3. about something you hope will happen today.

4. about a place that you see in your dreams.

5. about wildlife you saw.

6. about the best food you ever tasted.

7. about something that scared you.

8. about your favorite holiday.

9. about the best book you ever read.

10. about the worst book you read.

11. about an embarassing moment.

12. about a game you won.

13. about a skill you have learned.

14. about a contest you entered.

PREPARE and GIVE a SPEECH

*"A slip of the foot you may soon recover,
But a slip of the tongue
you may never get over."*   Benjamin Franklin

PUBLIC SPEAKING

Evaluation Form for Speeches and Readings

DIRECTIONS: Use this page for evaluation of speakers and readers in your group. Each member of the group should evaluate each other member of the group. This gives feedback from many listeners — rather than from just one listener and evaluator. This is helpful since listeners often react in different ways to the same speech or reading.

Each item of the evaluation is worth 10 points; perfect score is 50.

Speaker/Reader Name _____ Judge/Evaluator Name_____

Type of presentation (circle one)   Speech   Reading   Other_____

_____ Audience contact and audience control.

_____ Clarity of diction and pronunciation.

_____ Phrasing, pauses, speed of reading/speech — appropriate to selection.

_____ Poise and self-confidence of speaker, look of confidence.

_____ Appropriate mood or emotion for the selection.

Total points _____

Comments:

Speaker/Reader Name _____ Judge/Evaluator Name_____

Type of presentation (circle one)   Speech   Reading   Other_____

_____ Audience contact and audience control.

_____ Clarity of diction and pronunciation.

_____ Phrasing, pauses, speed of reading/speech — appropriate to selection.

_____ Poise and self-confidence of speaker, look of confidence.

_____ Appropriate mood or emotion for the selection.

Total points _____

Comments:

Speaker/Reader Name _____ Judge/Evaluator Name_____

Type of presentation (circle one)   Speech   Reading   Other_____

_____ Audience contact and audience control.

_____ Clarity of diction and pronunciation.

_____ Phrasing, pauses, speed of reading/speech — appropriate to selection.

_____ Poise and self-confidence of speaker, look of confidence.

_____ Appropriate mood or emotion for the selection.

Total points _____

Comments:

Student Projects - Ideas & Plans. © Leadership Publishers, 1994

Student Project

STUDENT : Matthew Winegardner

PROJECT: Stand-up Comedy Routine

DESCRIPTION:
First, Matt read about comedy. He found that people laugh at the unexpected unusual interpretations.

He practiced his routine. Then presented it to groups.

Matt Winegardner entertains his classmates with a comedy routine.

"I'd like to be a comedian . I don't know if I can make a living doing it. But, I sure like to do it. The more the audience laughs, the funnier I can get." reports Matt.

Matt has been planning and completing independent projects for about five years. He is currently in the fifth grade.

ADVERTISING

WATCH ADS AND COMMERCIALS ON TELEVISION.

STUDY MAGAZINE ADS.

VISIT AN AD AGENCY.

WHAT
DID
YOU
LEARN?

Advertising

Student Projects - Ideas & Plans. © Leadership Publishers,1994

COUPONS

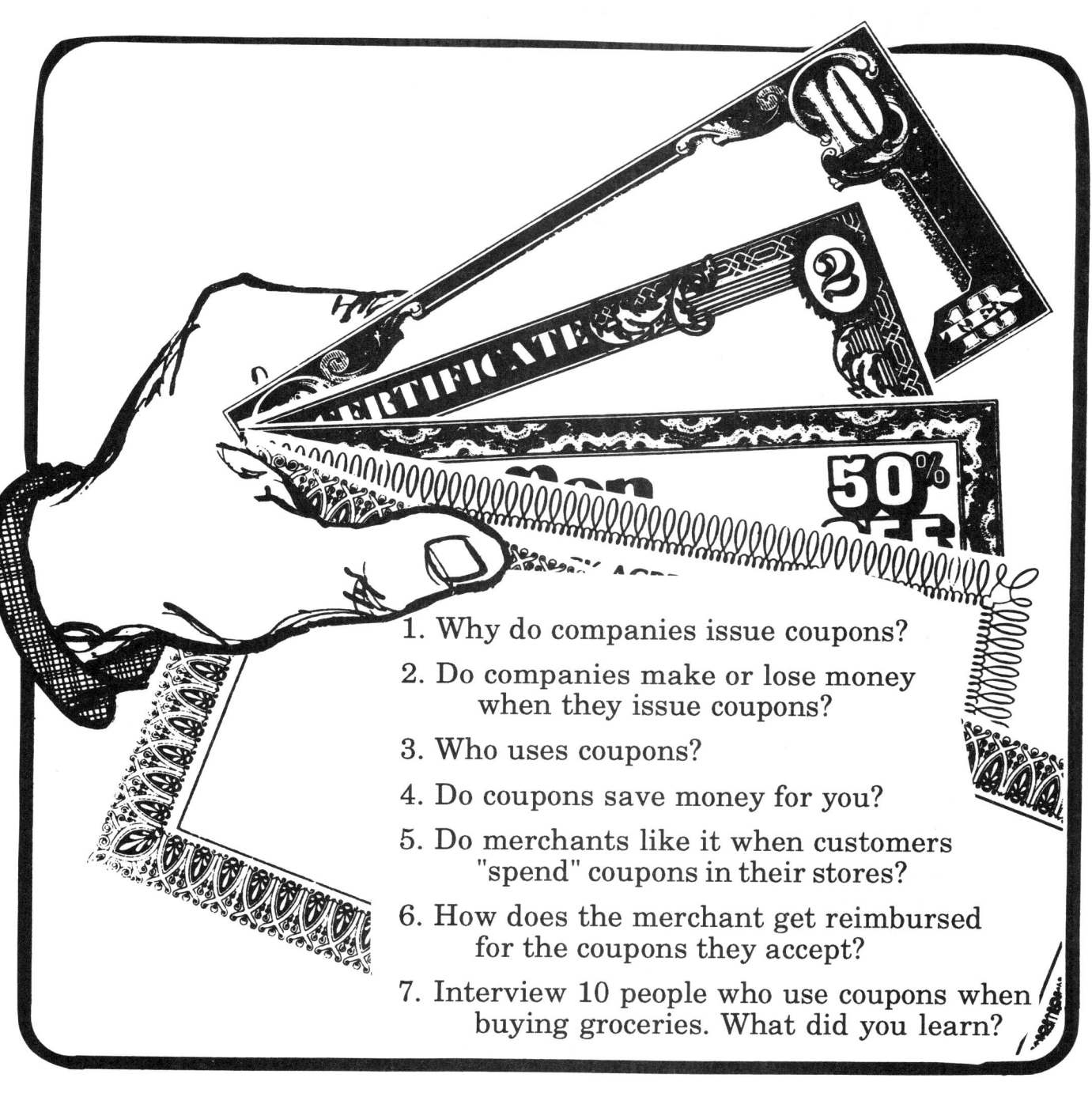

1. Why do companies issue coupons?

2. Do companies make or lose money when they issue coupons?

3. Who uses coupons?

4. Do coupons save money for you?

5. Do merchants like it when customers "spend" coupons in their stores?

6. How does the merchant get reimbursed for the coupons they accept?

7. Interview 10 people who use coupons when buying groceries. What did you learn?

DOLLS

1. Visit a doll museum.

2. Visit / interview someone who makes dolls.

3. Research different kinds of dolls - dolls that represent:

    √ periods of history,

    √ different careers,

    √ an event,

    √ a famous person,

    √ a fictional character,

    √ stages of life (baby....adult),

    √ dolls made from different materials:
       - cloth, ceramic, wood, corn husks, corn cob....

    √ famous doll makers.

4. Interview a psychologist, psychiatrist, policewoman, or medical doctor, to determine how dolls are used with children who are troubled or who have had an unpleasant experience.

5. Research: When are dolls considered antiques?

6. Write an essay about your favorite doll.

7. Put on a play in which your doll has the star role.

8. Hold a Doll Contest. You set the rules and prizes.

9. Is there a "Doll Clinic" in your area?
    A doll clinic is a place where dolls can be fixed.

Classify. . .

movies	plays	games
fruits	vegetables	diseases
military groups	weapons	spy activities
housing	household furniture	roofs
flowers	wires	grains
toys	cars	bikes
animals	reptiles	birds
sports	recreations	boats
gems	water	insects
tools	space	yarn
bears	tables	bells
beaks	bottles	bread
bridges	chairs	shapes
machines	shells	airplanes
costumes	wagons	dinosaurs
clothes	flags	clouds
glasses	pets	cameras
races	books	suitcases
puppets	fields	masks
art	bees	stoves
paint	rivers	lamps
sleds	cards	tanks
music	pies	webs

Songbirds

Songbirds are identified by size, beaks, feather shape and colors, flight and sound patterns, behavioral and food consumption habits, and the nests they build.

1. Locate and identify songbirds in your area.
   - ❏ Watch them.
   - ❏ Photograph them.
   - ❏ Draw them.
   - ❏ Chart their flight patterns.
   - ❏ Read about them.
   - ❏ Give someone a guided tour.

2. Study bird nests.
   Compare them for size, shape and building techniques and other variables.

3. Try to make a bird nest.

4. Research migratory habits of birds.

5. Draw a scale representing size of eggs - smallest to largest.

6. Visit your local or school library. How many bird books are there?

7. Invite an ornithologist to visit with you or your classroom.

Student Projects - Ideas & Plans. © Leadership Publishers,1994

1 Read about... *2* Make booklet about... *3* Build a bird feeder.
4 Make a word search using bird names. *5* Classify birds.

6 Give a report on a bird. *7* Listen to bird calls on records or tapes.

8 List extinct birds.

9 Read about Darwin's finches.

Birds

10 Read about the fabled Phoenix. *12* List birds of your area.
11 Study the various kinds of feathers on a bird.

13 Which birds have crests?

14 Essay: How Birds Help People

15 List birds that can be pets.

16 Describe the different kinds of bird beaks and bills.

17 Make a poster of bird pictures.

SPACE

Science fiction - what the world might be?

Timeline showing...

Future...?

Colonizing space...?

People who made history...

Fashions

1. Using 3 different years, do a comparative study of women's fashions. Describe:
   1) overall style
   2) hemline
   3) sleeves.

2. Why do people buy designer clothes? Do interviews.

3. Do a report, poster, lecture...on one or more well-known clothes designers.

4. This gown could belong in the movie "GONE WITH THE WIND". What other movies or stories could have gowns similar to the one pictured here?

Parasols

1. How are parasols made?

2. Collect different kinds of parasols. Give some history of each parasol. Review with 2 or more groups of people.

3. Design your own parasol to meet your own specific needs.

4. Host a "My Parasol Looks Like Me" contest. Participants will construct a parasol to match their personality/talents/unique characteristics.

Hats

1. What materials are commonly used to construct hats?

2. Make a poster of hats that identify occupations, example: firefighter's hat.

Fabric Adornments

Identify, read about, find samples of... materials and fabrics often used to adorn fabrics. Some examples are: lace, sequins...

ugly

silly

funny

the most

difficult

dear

challenging

satisfying

. . . . .

. . . . .

explore
the
WATERS

A story by

John Van Utrecht

TOM and *TERICA*

"Dad! Dad! Guess what?" said Dan.

"Sh-h-h-h. Quiet down. Your sister is sleeping."

Dad then spoke in a quiet voice. " Now, what were you going to say?"

"That female turkey hatched her eggs!"

"That's good. How many turkey poults are there?"

Dan said, "I counted five."

Dad, who always got excited when the turkey eggs hatched, said, " Well, let's go see how they are doing."

They went outside and, sure enough, there were five.

"Hey!" said Dan. "Why don't we name them?"

"Okay. Let's call that one Pete. That one Brad. That one Mike.

"What shall we call those two?" asked Dan. "How about TOM and TERICA?"

"Yes! I like those names. So, its settled. Their names are Pete, Brad, Mike, Tom and Terica. "

Then Dad turned to Dan and said, "Go get the poults some baby turkey feed."

Dan went and got some feed. When he was coming back, his father warned him to be careful. Female turkeys are very mean when they have babies.

So, when he went into the shed to feed the babies, he was very careful. He gave the poults their feed.

For a little bit the poults just stared at it. Then, after awhile, they finally ate some of it.

Time passed. The poults grew quickly. They had learned how to gobble. And they sure could gobble loudly! The Male turkeys pranced around the pen with all of their feathers sticking out.

Later, the Males got into fights. Usually, they would fight over a female.

Thanksgiving was coming up and Dan's father was sharpening his ax. Tom saw it. He asked his mother what it was for.

" What is the ax for, Mother?" Tom asked.

Tom Turkey's mother replied, "The man will chop your head off and eat you for Thanksgiving. "

Every turkey was running around in circles! "What will we do?" they cried.

"Calm down. I have a plan." reassured the mother turkey.

"Tell us," the young turkeys begged.

"This might not work but let's hope it does."

The young turkeys quieted down so they could hear their mother's plan.

"Now, here is my plan. Starting tomorrow, you, Tom, will watch and tell us when the farmer is coming. The rest of you, keep your ears open. When the farmer is coming, run outside. And when he comes in, quickly, everybody fly over the fence."

"Will we have to leave you forever?" asked Mike.

"I'm afraid so."

They cried a while, but their mother said, "It's either you run and fly away, or you die."

"Okay." they said.

Tom started watching for the farmer and the rest got ready. They waited awhile and finally Tom shouted. "Here he comes!"

So, everybody raced outside. The very minute the farmer stepped in, Tom and Terica jumped out. But the others weren't quick enough. They were caught!

Terica turned around and said, "Tom! Look! Our brothers are caught!"

"There's nothing we can do. We have to run," said Tom.

And away they went.

They kept on running until they came to a forest.

"It's sure dark in here," said Terica.

"I know." said Tom.

"We'll have to find a shelter because, any time now, I'm going to lay some eggs." said Terica.

"Oh, that is a problem," said Tom.

After quite a bit of looking, they found a dry riverbed that had been there a long time ago. The river had carved out the cave. Tom and Terica decided to live there.

They stayed in the cave, eating anything edible.

The time came for Terica to lay her eggs. She laid six eggs. She sat on them for a very , very, long time.

Finally to her surprise, all six of them hatched. Tom and Terica were very proud parents. Tom trotted around, acting like he owned the world.

All of the poults were very cute. It was a full time job for Tom and Terica getting all of the food. They took them for walks around the forest.

It was a peaceful life.

One day, they went up on a hill. Looking down, Terica said, "Just looking down brings back the old memories, doesn't it, Tom?"

"Yes, it does." said Tom. "Yes, it does."

The End

Use this flowchart (or similar plan) to plan and host a HOBBY FAIR for your class (school).

Hobby Fair

PROJECT GOAL
Host a Hobby Fair for your School.

SEQUENCE OF EVENTS	PERSON IN CHARGE	TASK DESCRIPTION
Chair Program Get all permissions		
Establish committees		
Establish rules for entries Post notices		
Publicity: teachers, press, students parents		
Prepare exhibit hall; check in exhibits – assign exhibit numbers		
Judging: which judges? criteria? awards?		
See that day run smoothly– supervise, etc.		

Additional Notes: _____

_____

_____

_____

HOBBY FAIR

Exhibit Number _____

EXHIBIT _____

GRADE _____

ENTERED BY _____

Judge Rating Sheet
HOBBY FAIR

Entry Number _____ Entry Name _____

Knowledge of Hobby (possible 10 points) _____

Value of Hobby to the exhibitor (possible 10 points) _____

Clarity of expression when speaking about hobby (possible 5 points) _____

Total points earned _____

COMMENTS:

Judge Rating Sheet
HOBBY FAIR

Entry Number _____ Entry Name _____

Knowledge of Hobby (possible 10 points) _____

Value of Hobby to the exhibitor (possible 10 points) _____

Clarity of expression when speaking about hobby (possible 5 points) _____

Total points earned _____

COMMENTS:

Judge Rating Sheet
HOBBY FAIR

Entry Number _____ Entry Name _____

Knowledge of Hobby (possible 10 points) _____

Value of Hobby to the exhibitor (possible 10 points) _____

Clarity of expression when speaking about hobby (possible 5 points) _____

Total points earned _____

COMMENTS:

Judge Rating Sheet
HOBBY FAIR

Entry Number _____ Entry Name _____

Knowledge of Hobby (possible 10 points) _____

Value of Hobby to the exhibitor (possible 10 points) _____

Clarity of expression when speaking about hobby (possible 5 points) _____

Total points earned _____

COMMENTS:

Shoes

Read about . . .
Classify . . .
Write a report on . . .
Interview someone who . . .
Compare one . . . to . . .
Hypothesize about . . .
Make a diorama of . . .
Take a field trip to . . .
Use a computer to . . .
Make a poster of . . .
Invent a . . .
Do a survey to find out . . .
Volunteer your services to . . .
Write a play . . .
Perform a play . . .
Write a song . . .
Sing a solo . . .
Form a musical group . . .
Collect oral history about . . .
Make a booklet of . . .
Draw a picture . . .
Collect . . .
Read poetry . . .
Write a poem . . .
Assemble a bibliography . . .
Write science fiction . . .
Write a fictional story . . .
Observe . . .
Experiment . . .
Write a letter to . . .
Redesign the . . .

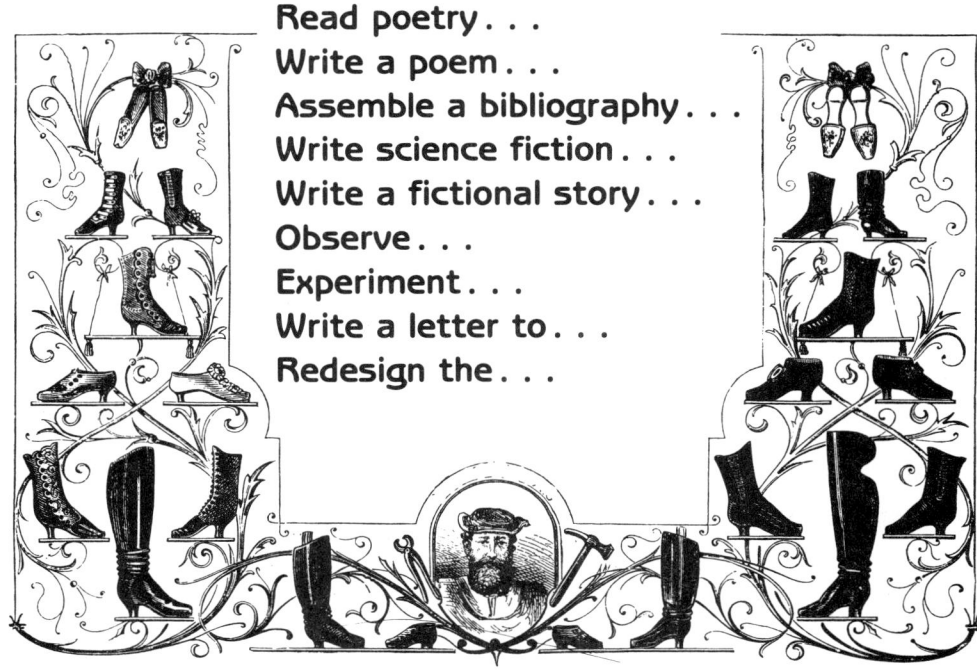

Time Zones

When it is 1:00 in your area _____ (your home),

it is 2:00 in: _____,

it is 3:00 in: _____,

it is 4:00 in: _____,

it is 5:00 in: _____,

Clocks

and

Timepieces

identify...
list...
report on...
read about...
collect...
design a new...

Write a story in which an hourglass or sundial play an important part in solving a mystery.

Make a crossword puzzle, or other word game, which uses clock or time-keeping terms.

Research calendars.

Design your own daily reminder calendar.

For one week, record what is happening at exactly 2:00 in the afternoon. Anything interesting?

Design a sundial. Set your sundial and a clock near each other in a place where the sun usually shines. Does your sundial tell accurate time? Use the clock to check your sundial.

At this present point in time, which watches are considered the:
a) most expensive
b) most prestigious
c) least expensive

New York

Read about . . .

Collect pictures of . . .

Investigate the history of . . .

List tourist attractions of . . .

Visit   . . .

Read about the city in an encyclopedia.

C I T I E S

CITIES

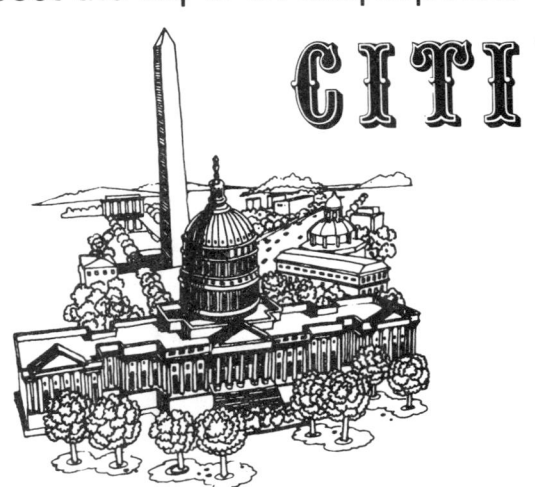

Washington

Houston

BIG

1. Read about the big cats.

2. Make a poster.

3. Identify all varieties of big cats.

4. Make a diorama showing big cats in their natural surroundings.

5. Make a set of cards. Draw a picture, or put the name of the big cat on one side. List facts about the big cat on the other side.

6. Read stories that feature a big cat. These stories can be fiction (made up) or nonfiction (based on true events or facts).

7. Construct a word search of big cats.

8. Watch a program on educational or public television about the big cats. List 10 facts you learned.

9. Compare habits of cats with habits of dogs.

10. Visit a zoo. How many big cats did you see? Be specific when naming of listing them.

CATS

Student Projects - Ideas & Plans. © Leadership Publishers, 1994

Quilts

Design a quilt with regular quilting patterns.

Design a crazy quilt - a quilt with irregular shapes.

Learn how to quilt.

Visit a quilt exhibit.

Interview someone who quilts.

List materials and supplies needed to quilt.

Read books about quilts.

National Anthems

1. What is your national anthem?

    Can you sing it?

    Can you play it on a musical instrument?

    Why was it selected?

    Who wrote it?

2. What is the purpose of a national anthem?

3. Research the national anthem of 10 or more countries.

    Write a report. Use a grid form for your report.

Example:

National Anthems	
Country	National Anthem
Canada	Oh, Canada
United States	Star-spangled Banner
France	Marseillaise

Ostrich

Some facts about ostriches:

1. Raising ostriches is a fast-growing business. They are raised for feathers, leather and meat.

2. Ostriches belongs to the Ratite family - a family of flightless birds.

3. An ostrich is the largest bird that we have seen and identified. It can weigh up to 450 pounds and be six feet tall.

4. Life expectancy is approximately 70 years.

More facts about ostriches:

5. 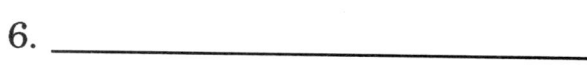 _____

_____

6. _____

_____

7. _____

_____

8. _____

_____

9. _____

_____

10. _____

_____

Student Projects - Ideas & Plans. © Leadership Publishers, 1994

Scavenger Hunts

Create a hunt:
- pick a theme
- write the clues
- award the prizes

Suggested themes:

- things of interest in the neighborhood,

- things that have certain colors

- cornerstones of buildings

- things that change colors

. . . . . .

Suggestions for writing the list:

- list actual names of objects

- give clues in code, rhyme, poetry

- create a map

- use several foreign languages

(add pictures for this one)

Have a fun, safe & friendly hunt!

Write an essay.

Student Project

The introductory paragraph is excellent for this type of writing.

Girls

My interest in girls has changed drastically over the past two years.

Two years ago, I did not like girls very much. I thought that they were kind of icky and not very nice. It was because they were kind of snobby and all stuck up, if you know what I mean. I tried to act and be nice, but they wanted no part of me.

Now, I like the girls a whole lot, but they still don't want any part of me. I try to be nice, but it just doesn't help.

I know what turns them off. It's my fat. They like a boy who is skinny and athletic. It is also my looks. There just is not one girl who likes me. I have even been turned down by the nobodies. I am worthless.

I wish one girl would like me. I like two or three girls a whole lot, but I just don't have the nerve to ask them if they will go with me.

The End.

MOTORCYCLES & BIKES

1. History of...

2. Competitions for...

3. How to learn to ride...

4. How these vehicles can be improved...

Write a letter to . . .

a friend   your grandmother   older brother or sister

neighbor who moved   a government leader   an author

a penpal   enter a contest   mail a coupon   a singer

Dear

National
Monuments

1. What are they?

2. Why were they built?

3. What do they represent?

4. When were they built?

5. Name 5 national monuments for your country.

6. Make a Trivia Game based on national monuments from many nations.

7. Draw a national monument.

8. Draw a scale-drawing of a national monument.

9. Make a scaled replica of a national monument.

10. "Interview" the monument. If the monument could talk, what might it answer to your questions?

11. Discuss: "Why are national monuments important to a country?"

12. Write a song or poem to honor a national monument.

Food Preservation

Why....?

How....?

Value of....?

Ways to:

- Drying
- Smoking
- Canning
- Pickling
- Freezing
- Jam & Jelly-making
- Cheese-making
- Sausage-making
- Butters & Sauce-making

Research... Learn how to.... Taste.... Watch demonstration of....

Herbs

PARSLEY

Herbs are useful plants.

1. Make a list of herbs.

2. Draw sketches of herbs.

3. Visit an herb garden. What did you see? What did you learn?

4. Grow an herb garden.

5. Research why herbs are used.
   Examples: scent, medicine, seasoning, flavoring, dyes.

6. Read recipes that accent specific herbs.
   If possible, prepare one or several of these recipes.

7. Research one specific herb. Include:

   a. where it is raised,

   b. what does it look like,

   c. what is its use,

   d. when was it first used as an herb,

   e. is the herb associated with a specific culture,
      Examples: curry-Indian dishes, Saffron-Cornish foods

   f. any special growing or using directions,

   g. how is the herb processed or packaged,

   h. compare costs of ounce of this herb with one ounce of
      three different herbs.

8. Write a play in which herbs describe their growing habits and use.

9. Other topic:

   _____

MINT

CHIVES

Herbs

STAMPS

A _stamp_ is an official mark or seal, or a small printed piece of paper with glue on one side.

1. Read the history of stamps and fees collected for stamps.

2. Learn how stamps are printed on one side and glued on the other.

3. Learn how stamps are designed.

4. Trace the history and cost of first-class postage stamps.

5. Visit a stamp collector. What did you learn?

6. Start a stamp collection.

7. Give a report on the tools, knowledge and sources of stamps that may be needed to be a stamp collector.

8. Research: _What makes stamps valuable?_

9. Research: _How are values placed on rare or unusual stamps?_

10. Research: _What kinds of paper, ink and printing processes are used to make stamps?_

11. Make a dictionary of terms associated with stamp collecting.

12. Visit the local post office. What new stamps are being issued in the near future?

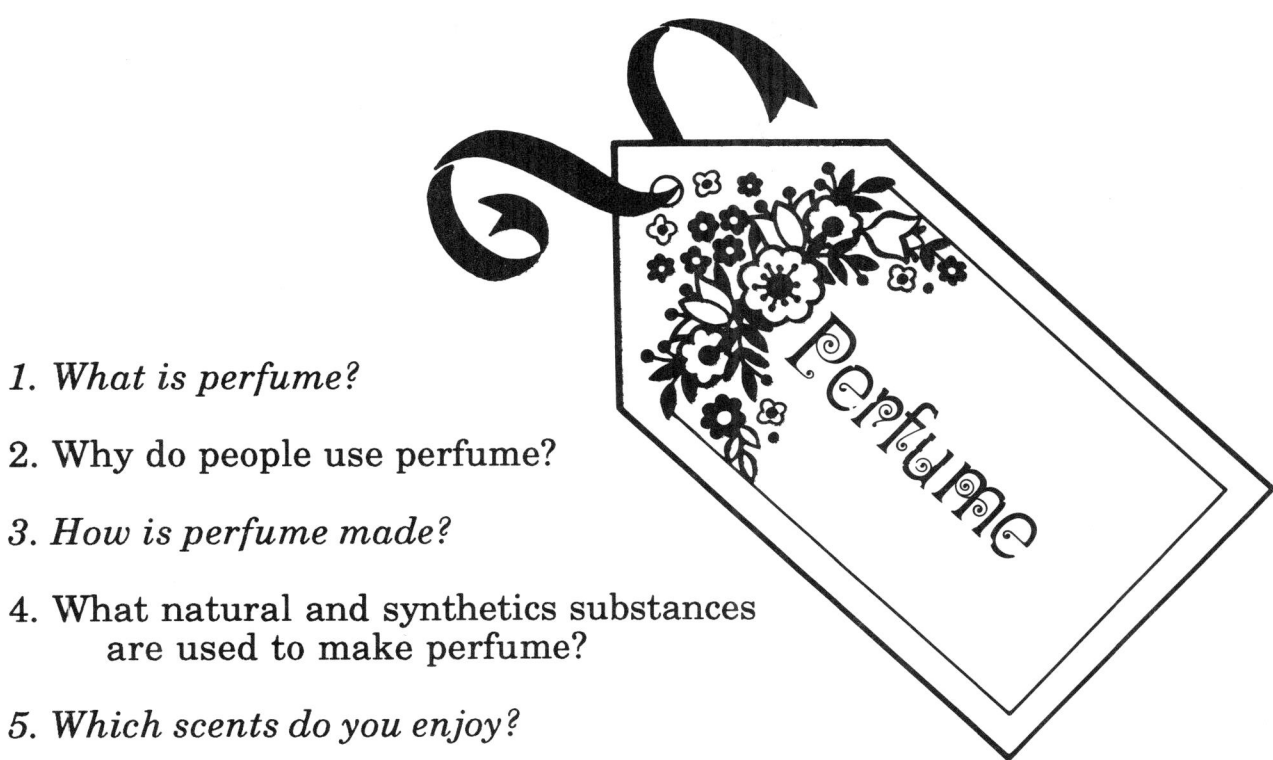

1. *What is perfume?*

2. Why do people use perfume?

3. *How is perfume made?*

4. What natural and synthetics substances are used to make perfume?

5. *Which scents do you enjoy?*

6. In perfume making, what do these terms mean:

    - essentials oils,

    - solvent extraction,

    - enfleurage?

7. *If you created a perfume, what name would you give it?*

8. Do you use perfume? Why or why not?

9. *Do you like it when others use perfume? Why or why not?*

10. Why are some perfumes inexpensive and others very expensive?

11. *Visit a store that sells perfume. Compare scents and prices. What did you learn?*

12. How many perfumes can you name? Besides the name of the perfume, what other information do you know about it?

13. *Which scents bring back memories for you?*

Student Projects - Ideas & Plans. © Leadership Publishers, 1994

RODEO

1. Attend a rodeo. Take pictures.
Explain to others what you saw and heard.

2. Make a dictionary of terms associated with the rodeo.

3. Interview someone who competes in rodeo events.

4. Read magazine articles or watch a rodeo
on television. What did you see and learn.
Would you like to compete in a rodeo event?

5. Research:
Study one event. How
did that event come
to be?

6. Report:
Study one event.
Learn and
report the
rules for
that
event.

7. Are there
rodeos in your
area?
Why <u>or</u> why not?

Student Projects - Ideas & Plans. © Leadership Publishers,1994

MUSIC

1. Read the history of
   a particular musical instrument.

2. Prepare and perform a musical solo.

3. Listen to a musical form which
   you have not regularly heard.
   *Examples: chorus, brass quintet,
   opera, symphony or others.*

4. Keep a diary of all music
   listened to in one week.

5. Survey your classmates. What
   is their favorite music?
   Who are their favorite musicians?

6. If you could learn to play one
   musical instrument, which would it be? Why?

7. Discuss this quotation
   "Music is a universal language."

8. Play a tape or record of your favorite
   music. Pretend you are singing or
   directing the music.

9. Visit a recording studio.
   What did you learn from the visit?

10. Make a crossword or word puzzle
    with entries of musicians,
    compositions, and musical terms.

11. Experiment: while listening to music,
    close your eyes. Does this enhance
    your ability to hear the music?

TEACH
a
SKILL

PROGRESS

1. Make a timeline to show improvements in a particular area, such as medicine, transportation...

2. Make a chart showing progress in space travel, food storage, or another topic.

3. Make a collage (similar to the one shown above) about progress.

4. Make a list of all areas that need to progress. Be as specific as possible about areas, ideas, and products that need to be improved.

faces and gestures

turtle

dog

Observe...

and report observations.

child

hands

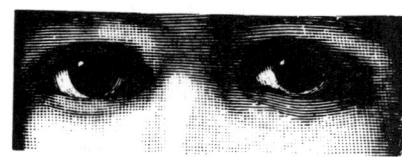

eyes

beauty of nature

Read about . . .
Classify . . .
Write a report on . . .
Interview someone who . . .
Compare one . . . to . . .
Hypothesize about . . .
Make a diorama of . . .
Take a field trip to . . .
Use a computer to . . .
Make a poster of . . .
Invent a . . .
Do a survey to find out . . .
Volunteer your services to . . .
Write a play . . .
Perform a play . . .
Write a song . . .
Sing a solo . . .
Form a musical group . . .
Collect oral history about . . .
Make a booklet of . . .
Draw a picture . . .
Collect . . .
Read poetry . . .
Write a poem . . .
Assemble a bibliography . . .
Write science fiction . . .
Write a fictional story . . .
Observe . . .
Experiment . . .
Write a letter to . . .
Redesign the . . .
Interpret . . .
Translate . . .
. . . other . . .

POND
LIFE

Student Projects - Ideas & Plans. © Leadership Publishers, 1994

Juke Box

Research the history of juke boxes.

Learn how a juke box operates.

Interview people who like juke boxes.

What is the value of an antique juke box?
- What determines the value of an antique?

1. Look at the pictures of dogs shown on this page. Identify the dogs.

2. Classify dogs using at least three classifications:
   a) tasks dogs often performed,   b) size,   c) disposition,   d) .....

3. Compare 10 dogs. Points of comparison:
   a) size, b) disposition, c) type of hair, d) color, e) ......

4. Write a story about a real dog. The story may be fictitious.

5. Research and report about a specific topic, such as: training dogs,
   seeing-eye dogs, sheep dogs, guard dogs, lap dogs, ...

6. It is sometimes said that people select dogs that look like them. Take
   photographs of dogs and their masters. Do the two look alike?

7. Discuss: *"Civilization progressed because man and dog became friends."*

Three Ambitious Students:

Jennifer Siasoco, Trisha Knox, Amanda Green
Des Moines, Iowa

Independent projects completed by these three students in <u>one</u> school year.

Jennifer Siasoco	Trisha Knox	Amanda Green
History of the Philippines	Japan: A Report	My Special Places
Reading is Fun	Creative Writings - Collection	Famous People
Story (fiction)	Drawings - Collection	Flashcards
Des Moines: A Report	Hawaiian Picture	Valentine Poster
		Des Moines: A Report
		Netherlands: A Report

Jennifer, Trisha and Amanda also completed several group projects:

Zoo Picture, Christmas Play, Circus Picture, Fashions,
Haunted House Play, Newspaper, Awards.

Good Work, Students!

Student Projects - Ideas & Plans. © Leadership Publishers, 1994

Peace

1. How do you define peace?
   Do others agree with your definition?

2. Why is peace so difficult?

3. List 3 (or more) steps <u>you</u> can take
   to bring about world peace.

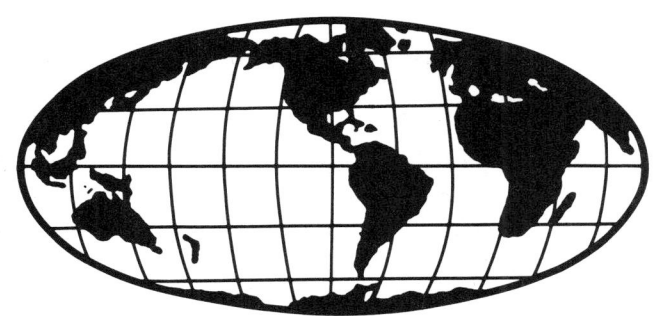

What is an

Idea ?

Where does it come from?

Gardens

Take your choice:

- ☞ describe
- ☞ read about
- ☞ visit
- ☞ design
- ☞ enjoy

the different kinds of gardens

- ⇨ fruit garden
- ⇨ vegetable garden
- ⇨ flower garden
- ⇨ cactus garden
- ⇨ butterfly garden
- ⇨ water garden
- ⇨ _____ garden.

Write a song. . .

Sing a solo. . .

Student Projects - Ideas & Plans. © Leadership Publishers, 1994

Mascots

Part One.

List 5 qualities that make a good mascot (symbol):

1. _____

2. _____

3. _____

4. _____

5. _____

Part Two.

List 10 or more mascots and the team or company each represents.

1. Mascot _____ represents _____.

2. Mascot _____ represents _____.

3. Mascot _____ represents _____.

4. Mascot _____ represents _____.

5. Mascot _____ represents _____.

6. Mascot _____ represents _____.

7. Mascot _____ represents _____.

8. Mascot _____ represents _____.

9. Mascot _____ represents _____.

10. Mascot _____ represents _____.

Video:

- **Learn to use a video recorder.**
- **Select a topic. Make a video about it.**

. . . . other projects of your choice.

Draw a picture. . .

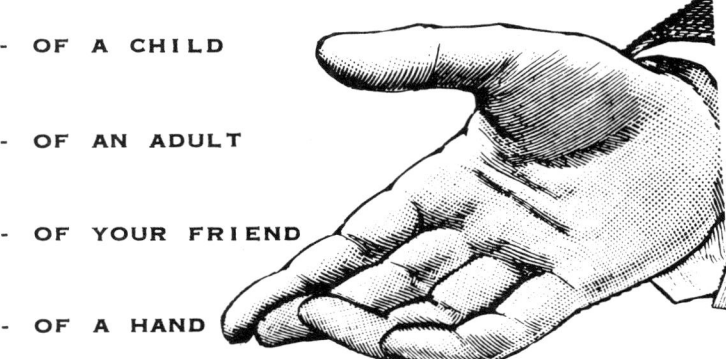

- OF A LEAF

- OF A CHILD

- OF AN ADULT

- OF YOUR FRIEND

- OF A HAND

- OF A SUNSET

- OF A DOG

- OF A CAT

- OF YOUR PET

- OF A CHAIR

- OF A TREE

- OF A BOOKCASE

- OF A DOOR

- OF STAIRS

- OF A STORM

- OF A BOWL OF FRUIT

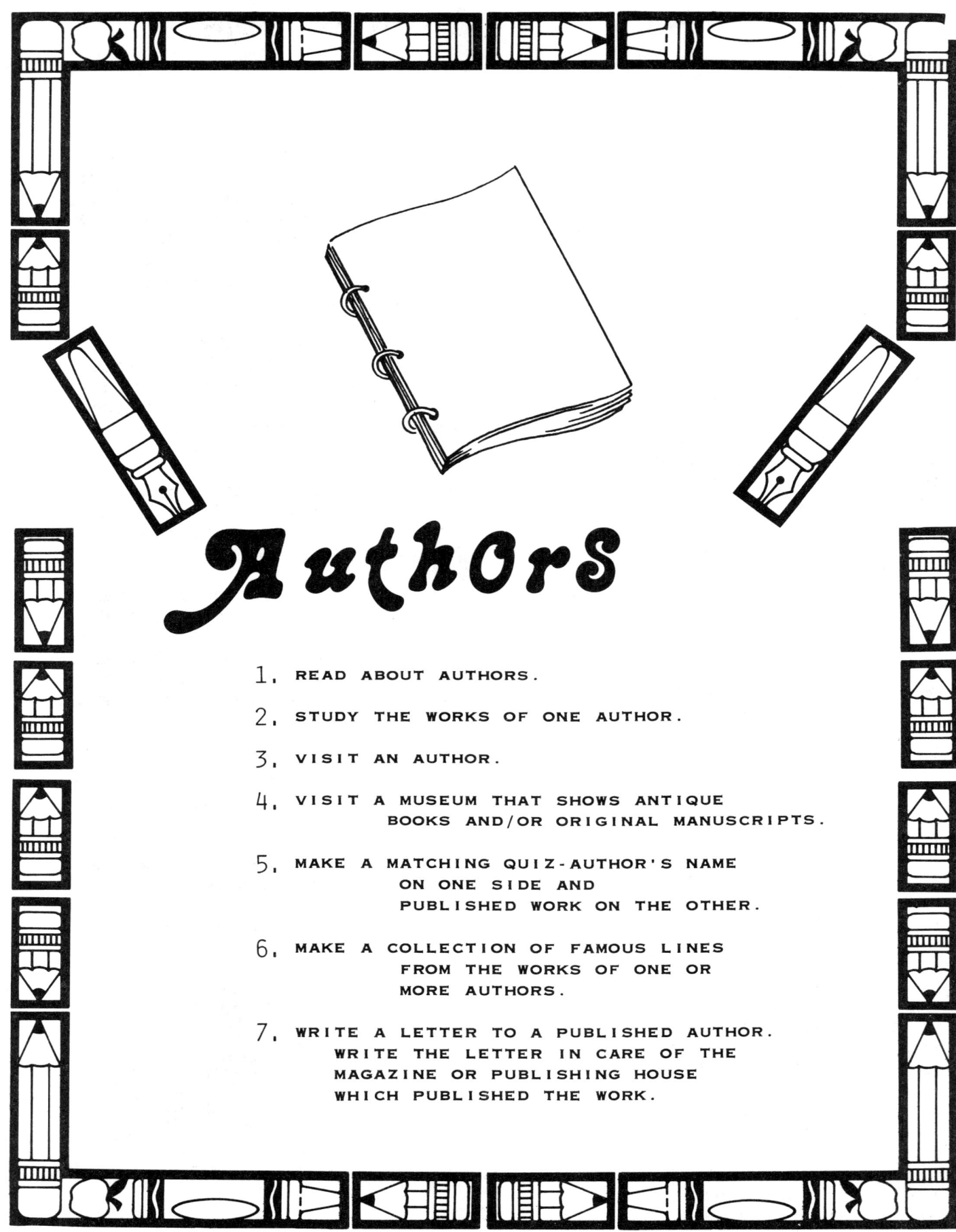

Authors

1. READ ABOUT AUTHORS.

2. STUDY THE WORKS OF ONE AUTHOR.

3. VISIT AN AUTHOR.

4. VISIT A MUSEUM THAT SHOWS ANTIQUE BOOKS AND/OR ORIGINAL MANUSCRIPTS.

5. MAKE A MATCHING QUIZ-AUTHOR'S NAME ON ONE SIDE AND PUBLISHED WORK ON THE OTHER.

6. MAKE A COLLECTION OF FAMOUS LINES FROM THE WORKS OF ONE OR MORE AUTHORS.

7. WRITE A LETTER TO A PUBLISHED AUTHOR. WRITE THE LETTER IN CARE OF THE MAGAZINE OR PUBLISHING HOUSE WHICH PUBLISHED THE WORK.

Student Project

Going Camping

Kim, Tom, Sarah and James were going camping. While they were at school, all they could think about was going camping. Over the week, they had planned what to bring.

Tom was bringing the kettle. Kim was bringing the food, because she was the oldest, and knew how to cook. James was bringing the tent and fishing pole. Sarah was bringing the sleeping bags. No matter what, they were going camping.

They had all got to bed early the night before the great day.

Finally the big day came. They were awake when it started to get light. By the time it started to get dark at night, they had found a place to camp for the night.

Kim fixed the food. James, with a little help from Tom, was setting up the tent.

When the tent was set up, Sarah put the sleeping bags in the tent. When everything was ready, they ate and went to sleep.

It happened in the night. They didn't know exactly what time it was. All they knew was that it was dark - pitch black! The noise was quiet at first. They thought it was just the wind blowing through trees. But then, they listened closer. It didn't sound like the wind.

Tom volunteered to go outside since he was the oldest and, he thought, the bravest.

Tom came back and told them all to put on their jackets. An owl had become entangled in some old bailing wire. The noise they heard was the owl trying to get loose. As he flapped his wings, the wire hit against some junk and the steel posts of the fence.

Very carefully, Tom held the wings of the frightened owl. Knowing that the owl's talons were very sharp, Sarah and Kim put on gloves before they carefully removed the owl's feathered feet from the wire.

After its release, the owl quickly and silently flew off. The campers were proud of their efforts to save the mighty owl.

By the time all the excitement of the owl was over, James said, " We might as well get up. See? The sky is starting to get light. That means that the sun is only about 30 minutes away. We better go catch some fish for our breakfast."

They went fishing for their breakfast. When they got back to the tent, Kim fried the fish. They ate the fish.

After breakfast they packed up everything and went home.

Camping was really fun!

Create a GAME based on the geography of North America.

Problem Solving

We hate to BUG you, but . . . MOST PROBLEMS HAVE AT LEAST ONE SOLUTION. FIND IT.

Directions: List something that "bugs" (bothers) you.
Then list one possible solution.

THIS 'BUGS' (BOTHERS) ME   **ONE SOLUTION**

_____   _____

_____   _____

_____   _____

_____   _____

_____   _____

_____   _____

Host: **Summertime Opportunities**

Here is a sample:

Summertime Opportunities

Rules

1. Students must have completed kindergarten as of May of this year. Next year's incoming kindergarten and this year's outgoing seniors are not eligible.

2. Projects must be started, or the greater percentage of the project completed, after school is dismissed for the year.

3. Projects and entries must be brought to school by _____ (date).

4. Students may enter as many categories as they wish to enter.

5. Decisions by the judges are final.

6. The committee assumes students are honest.

Categories

1. Most pages read. Keep track of the number of pages and submit the total.

2. Most interesting poem.

3. Most interesting story (entry must be legible or it will be disqualified).

4. Collection of 3 or more pencil sketches.

5. Collection of 3 or more ink sketches or drawings.

6. Open category for art projects (painting, sculpture....)

7. Cartoon. Develop sequence of frames or single frame with caption.

8. Invention - it must work.

9. Original song. It may be submitted on paper, tape or in person.

10. Travelogue of a trip taken.

11. Diary for summertime. It must cover at least one week: entries for 7 or more consecutive days.

12. Photography - people and their activities.

13. Photography - world about us (pictures where people are not the main point of interest). These could be events, animals, plants, ...

14. Design an original computer program. Submission is by computer disk.

15. Open category for anything that reflects individual thinking, innovation and productivity. This covers ideas not covered in previous listings. The decisions of the judges are final.

Committee members: - *list them.*

Submit entries to _____ (location).

Have a great summer!

Student Projects - Ideas & Plans. © Leadership Publishers, 1994

Design a Playground that reflects your community.

Will it have trees?

tractors?

tires?

swings?

ramps?

grass?

water?

.....?

.....?

.....?

Sketch it.

LOGO

Ireland

Combine

several drawings

that represent your

town or community,

state or province,

and your country.

Canada

Gems, Jewels and Jewelry

1. What is a gem? jewel?

2. What is jewelry?

3. What are the "Crown Jewels"?

4. List precious and semiprecious stones.

5. What are imitation or artificial gems? How are they made? What is their value?

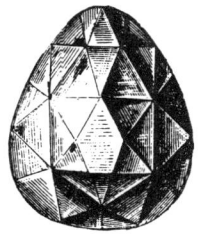

6. Read the history about famous gems.
   Examples: La Pellegrina (pearl),
   Hope Diamond (diamond)

7. To determine the value of a gem, these factors must be considered: hardness, color, brilliance, rarity, and demand. Using these standards, which gems are most valuable today?

8. Write a mystery in which a gem plays an important role.

9. Visit a jewelry store. Visit with a jeweler about the current price of gems.

10. If you could have any gem or jewel, which would it be? Why?

 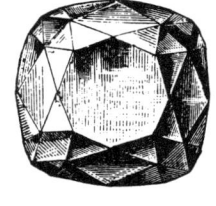 

Radio

How does a radio work?

Do you listen to the radio?
- news?
- music?
- radio dramas?
- sports?

Do you listen to public or commercial radio?

How has the radio changed over the years?

What role does the radio play in:
- a democracy?
- a crisis?
- everyday life?

What is violence?

Are you violent?

Have you been the victim of violence?

Are your friends violent?

Have your friends been the victims of violence?

Is violence increasing or decreasing?
Support your reasons with examples.

What is to be done:
- personally,
- socially,
- religiously,
- legally,
- ....

VIOLENCE

Rainforest

Draw a rainforest.

Umpires, Referees, and Judges.

Directions:
All of the people listed in the title make decisions or pass judgments.
1. Illustrate the people. 2. Can you add to this list of decision makers?

Weather Events

Volcanoes:
    -famous volcanoes
    -formation of
    - _____

Earthquakes:
    -famous earthquakes
    - formation of
    -measuring

    - _____

Floods:
    -famous floods in your area
    -reasons why rivers flood
    -effects of floods ⟨ desirable
                        not-desirable

    - _____

Hurricanes:
    - famous hurricanes
    - formation of
    -measuring
    - effects of

    - _____

Other weather events:

_____

Student Projects - Ideas & Plans. © Leadership Publishers,1994

Student Project

S T U D E N T: Michele Bond, *grade One*

P R O J E C T: Reading to a Mentor

D E S C R I P T I O N: Michele is an avid first-grade reader. She is released from some classroom time to read with a mentor. The mentor listens to her read, explains the meaning of new words, and discusses (when Michele wants to) the content of what she has read.

M E N T O R: Mr. Roets, another teacher on the staff.

Shown here are Michele Bond and her mentor, Mr. Roets.

Michele says, "I like to read. I read all the time."

Reading

Student Projects - Ideas & Plans. © Leadership Publishers, 1994

Book Titles

Directions: Select one or more of these book titles. Write a brief summary of the contents, plot and conflict of a story that may have that title.

Peanuts and Popcorn

Secret Vitamins; Secret Power

Unpredictable Uncle Ernest

Just Be My Friend

Will You Love Me If I Fail?

How Far Away Is Home?

Red Carnations in the Winter

Okay? No Way!

Pappa's Pizza Powwow

New Teacher — New Challenge

Get Lost and Leave Me Alone

Chocolate Sundae Sunday

Want to Share My Candy Bar?

Kid Brothers Are For Ignoring

I Hate Pink Medicine

Mud Pies in March

Locker Room Wars

Luke's Lawn Cutting Business

Sara Tells the Funniest Jokes

School's O.K. Except on Monday

Rotten Apples and Ripe Tomatoes

Student Projects - Ideas & Plans. © Leadership Publishers, 1994

Student **SHARON ROUW** *used book title*
RED CARNATIONS IN THE WINTER *to develop this story plot.*

Student Project

RED CARNATIONS IN THE WINTER will be a story about a brother and sister. Their parents were killed in a car accident. He is older and in college. She is a senior in high school. Each year he sends red carnations for her birthday.

This year, he, too is killed in an accident. But, because the red carnations have been ordered, they arrive on her birthday.

Her first reaction is to throw the flowers away. Then she reconsiders.

The carnations become the symbol of hope and courage. They speak a message from her brother: *"Your life must go on."*

Red Carnations in the Winter

Television

1. Which inventor(s) invented television?

2. Make up a question & answer game based on the programs currently on television.

3. Interview a person who hosts of co-hosts a television show. What do you want to ask?

4. Write a series for television.

5. Research how many minutes of program and how many minutes of advertising are in a 30-minute TV program.

6. Survey your classmates. Which television program is their favorite?

7. How would you suggest that television be improved?

8. Within your lifetime, how has television changed?

9. Write a story line for your favorite television show.

10. Why is your favorite television show your favorite television show?

11. *Your choice:* _____

_____

Student Projects - Ideas & Plans. © Leadership Publishers, 1994

CARS

1. Read about the history of cars and other land vehicles.

2. Research topic: Which cars are now considered the most-valued antique cars?

3. Which movies use special car models?

4. Improve the current car designs.

5. Complete this sentence: *"My ideal car..."*

6. Complete this sentence: *"Cars of the future will..."*

Cars

Balloons

your choice

Student Projects - Ideas & Plans. © Leadership Publishers, 1994

Complete this design

Foods

1. Study and demonstrate the main food groups.

2. Keep a diary of everything you eat - for three days. Are you getting a balanced diet?

3. Organize an ethnic food fair. Prepare recipes from various ethnic groups. Share the food with others.

4. Read about, purchase and sample food not readily eaten in our community. Report to the rest of your class.

5. Investigate how companies and states promote specialty foods.

   Examples: Wisconsin - cheese
   Iowa - Iowa pork chop
   Maine - lobsters

6. Collect recipes and menus from restaurants around the country, and if possible, the world. Compare them. (If you cannot obtain the actual menu, perhaps you will find menus published in magazines.)

7. Investigate: What are the favorite foods of the current president or prime minister of your country?

8. What role does government play in the introduction and approval of unusual foods?

122

MUSHROOMS

1. What are mushrooms?

2. How do mushrooms grow?

3. What kinds of mushrooms are edible?

4. Which mushrooms are poisonous?

5. Collect recipes which require mushrooms.

6. Interview someone who collects edible mushrooms. Where do they find them?

7. What fairy and folk tales are associated with mushrooms?

8. Pick a mushroom. Look at it under a microscope. Let it dry. Study it again under the microscope or magnifying class.

9. Write a story in which a mushroom plays a part.

10. Are mushrooms and toadstools the same?

Write a report on . . .

ANY TOPIC OF YOUR CHOICE

(The pictures may suggest ideas.)

Candid Shots of Students

Rynee Lane

Students smile for the camera. Each student pictured here participated in and completed many student projects.

A partial list of their accomplishments:

√ Plays: writing & performing;

√ Writing fiction and nonfiction;

√ Skills mastery: library, research, word processing, computer programming;

√ Art: sculpture, drawing, sketching, illustrating, appreciation;

√ Committee work: Hobby Fair, Summertime Activities, Science Fair;

√ Competitions: Future Problem Solving, Odyssey of the Mind, Forensic;

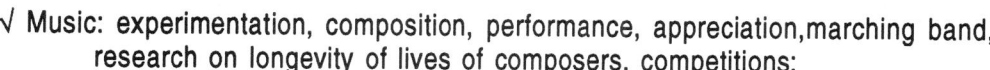

Darcie Dop

√ Music: experimentation, composition, performance, appreciation,marching band, research on longevity of lives of composers, competitions;

√ Posters: high tech machines, musicians, famous women, animals, solar system;

....and other areas of opportunity and interest.

Brandy LaRue

Sara Lanphier

Roxanne Lane

Brandon Yoder

Joe Strobel, James Howard, Matt Winegardner, Jennifer Alexander, Jodi Hicks

Bed & Breakfast

Bed & Breakfast (B&B) lodgings are becoming more and more popular. The owner of the B&B selects an appropriate house/home. One or severals rooms are prepared for guests. The rooms are rented by the night - similar to hotels and motels. A speciality breakfast is included in the price.

Each B&B has a particular style or focus. This style or focus will be reflected in the manner of room furnishings and breakfast provided. The name of the B&B will flow from the house name or its owners, location of the building, or a historic period in which the house was built.

The B&B's are a wonderful way to preserve some of our historic places. They are also a creative outlet for entrepreneurs, innkeepers, historians, antique collectors, and gourmet cooks.

Directions: Design a Bed & Breakfast (B&B).

Picture of the building (actual picture or sketch):

Geographic location: _____

Name of B&B: _____

Describe one bedroom: _____

_____

_____

Breakfast: _____

_____

_____

If you need help, check out a <u>Directory of Bed and Breakfasts</u>.
You will get ideas by looking at the pictures and reading descriptions.

Vampires, Ghouls

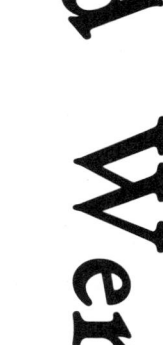

1. Define: *ghoul, vampire, werewolf.*

2. Give the history or use of each term listed in No. 1.

3. Write an essay that begins with this sentence:
   *"People like to read stories about ghouls, vampires,
   and werewolves because...."*

4. Make a bibliography of stories in which there are
   werewolves, vampires or ghouls. You may
   add other types of unusual creatures to this list.

5. List superstitions that cause people to fear the unknown.
   Example: ordinary person changing into a werewolf.

6. Write an essay on this topic:
   *"Werewolves, vampires and ghouls satisfy
   man's desire for the unusual."*

7. Create a new "monster". Give <u>it</u> a birth,
   mode of operation, and include it in a story.

8. Defend or negate this thesis:
   *"People must have monsters to control if they
   are to control their daily fears."*

9. Defend or negate this thesis:
   *"People created monsters as outlets for
   their own agressiveness."*

Your choice: _____

_____

Opera

1. Attend the opera.

2. Make a matching test: <u>composer</u> on one side and <u>opera title</u> on the other.

3. Make a dictionary of opera terms.

4. Make summaries of opera stories.

5. Listen to certain parts of operas:
   examples: overtures, choruses, duets ...

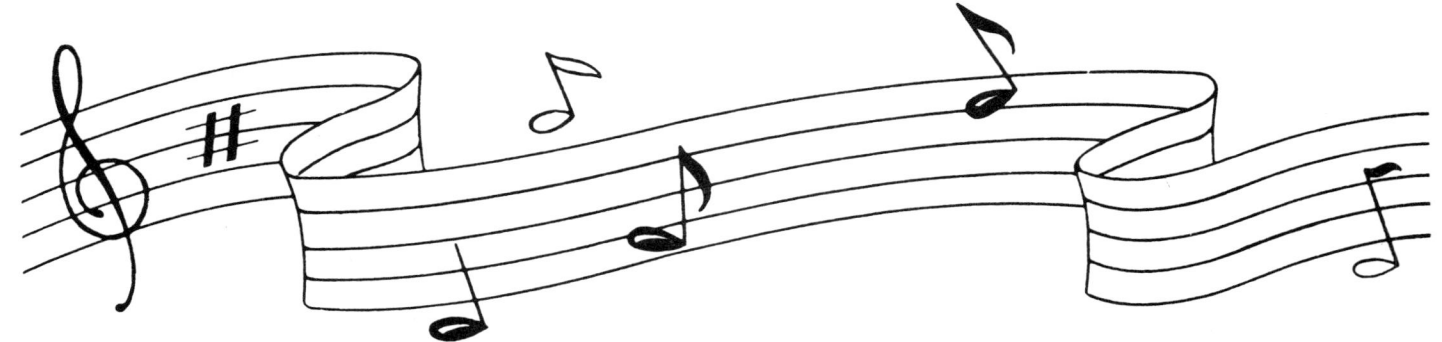

Read about . . .
Classify . . .
Write a report on . . .
Interview someone who . . .
Compare one . . . to . . .
Hypothesize about . . .
Make a diorama of . . .
Take a field trip to . . .
Use a computer to . . .
Make a poster of . . .
Invent a . . .
Do a survey to find out . . .
Volunteer your services to . . .
Write a play . . .
Perform a play . . .
Write a song . . .
Sing a solo . . .
Form a musical group . . .
Collect oral history about . . .
Make a booklet of . . .
Draw a picture . . .
Collect . . .
Read poetry . . .
Write a poem . . .
Assemble a bibliography . . .
Write science fiction . . .
Write a fictional story . . .
Observe . . .
Experiment . . .
Write a letter to . . .
Redesign the . . .
Interpret . . .
Translate . . .
. . . other . . .

wild
life

MAGIC

Optical illusions

Sleight of hand

Harry Houdini

1. MAKE A MODEL OF YOUR IDEAL HOME OR CABIN.

2. READ REAL ESTATE ADS IN MANY DIFFERENT MAGAZINES. WHAT DID YOU LEARN ABOUT THE VALUE OF PROPERTY

3. GIVEN YOUR CHOICE, WHERE WOULD YOU LIVE? IN WHAT TYPE OF HOUSE? WHY?

REAL ESTATE

The School Bus

1. Keep a diary of memories associated with riding the school bus.

2. Write a play that takes place on the school bus.

3. Keep a notebook of interesting bits of conversation heard on a school bus.

4. Write a report on your school bus: size, route description and other interesting information.

5. From your observations, how would you describe people who ride the same school bus as you ride.

Student Projects - Ideas & Plans. © Leadership Publishers,1994

Read about . . . Alphabets

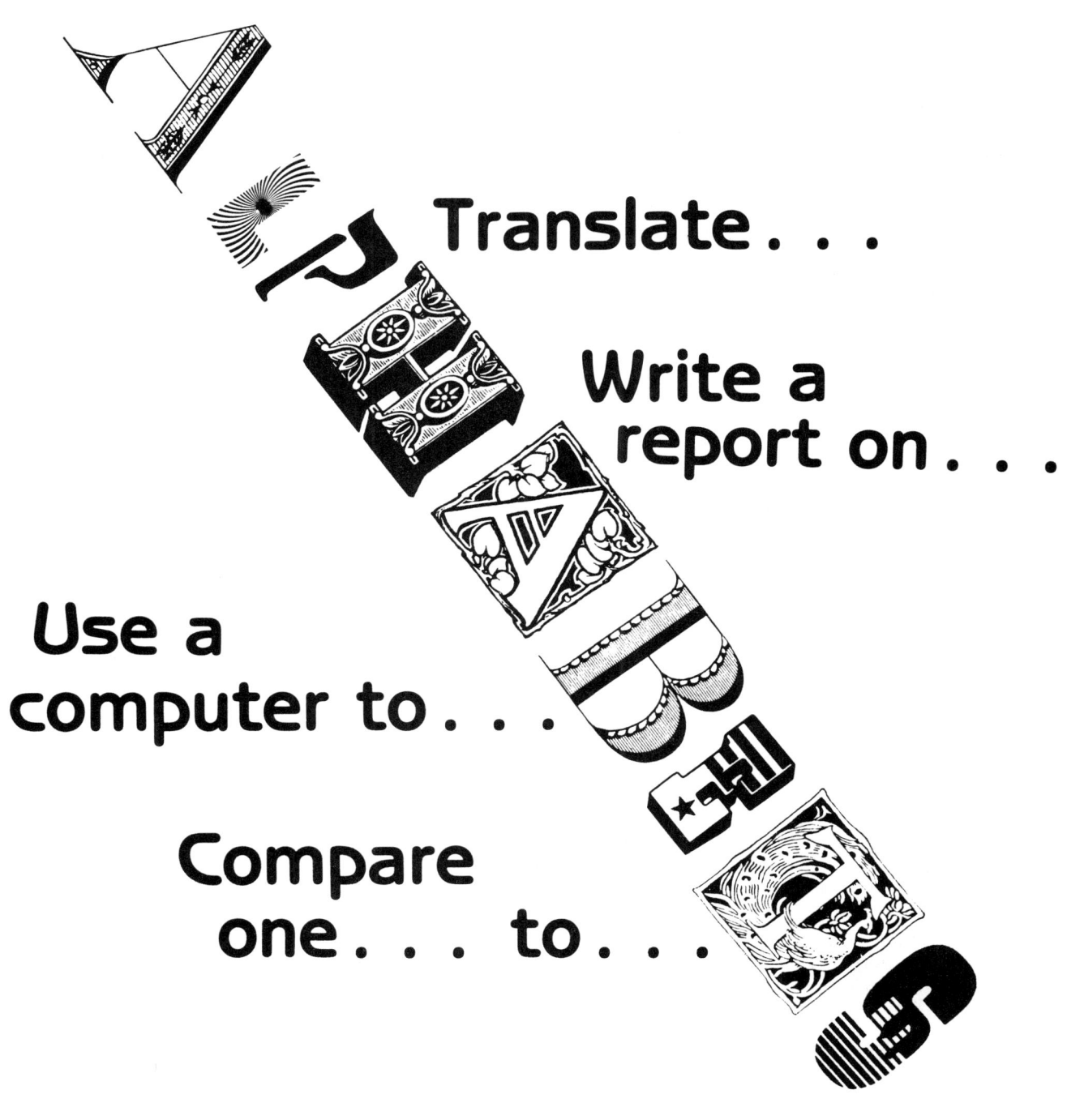

Translate . . .

Write a
report on . . .

Use a
computer to . . .

Compare
one . . . to . . .

Book Plates

BOOK MARKER is used to help the reader remember how far he or she has read.

BOOK PLATE is an identification label affixed to the book. A <u>book plate</u> lists the owner of the book.

Directions: Design your own <u>book marker</u> or <u>book plate</u>.

Reproduce copies. Use them. Share with friends.

134

Memo & Note Pads

Design a notepad or memo pad.
Your notepad should reflect your personality or likes.

FROM THE DESK OF

*Angela is in 10th grade.
She's been writing
poetry for many years.*

Author:
ANGELA   SHEESLEY

As Summer Ends

The end of summer is a magic time.

To some, it is relieving the heat.
To others, it is regretting the cold.

My summer's end is a sad time:
The end of lying in the sun-
Catching it's bright, warm rays,
Swimming in cool lakes and pools,
Running on the hot, baking sand,
Vacation and summer romances,
New people from far away-
Maybe never to be seen again,
Sunburnt noses and shoulders,
Darkly tanned legs and arms,
Feet without any shoes on,
Camping in tents and fishing for big fish,
Warm nights with crickets chirping,
Light blankets and cool sheets,
Shorts, tank tops, and swimming suits,
Bleached hair from the golden sun,
Sleeping the morning 'til afternoon.

As they say "Where does the summer go?"

If I knew, would I follow it?
Then summer would never end,
And fall would never begin.

Student Projects - Ideas & Plans. © Leadership Publishers,1994

Leisure

Time

Carnival

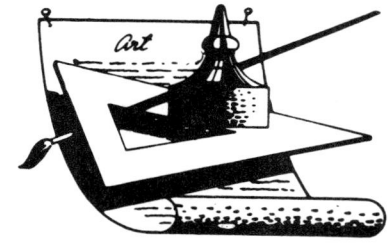

Art

Quirks,
Quarks,

and other

things and words

that start with

Qu.......

Qu_____

Qu_____

Qu_____

Qu_____

Qu_____

Qu_____

Qu_____

Qu_____

Qu_____

Qu_____

Qu_____

Qu_____

Albatross,   A_____

Alligator,   A_____

Abalone   A_____

and other   A_____

animals   A_____

associated with   A_____

water.   A_____

Food

Junk

Good

Observe . . .

Perform a play . . .

Redesign the . . .

Write a play . . .

Do a survey to find out . . .

Redesign the . . .

Invent a . . .

Experiment . . .

Write science fiction . . .

Write a letter to . . .

Write a fictional story . . .

Collect history about . . .

Write a song . . .

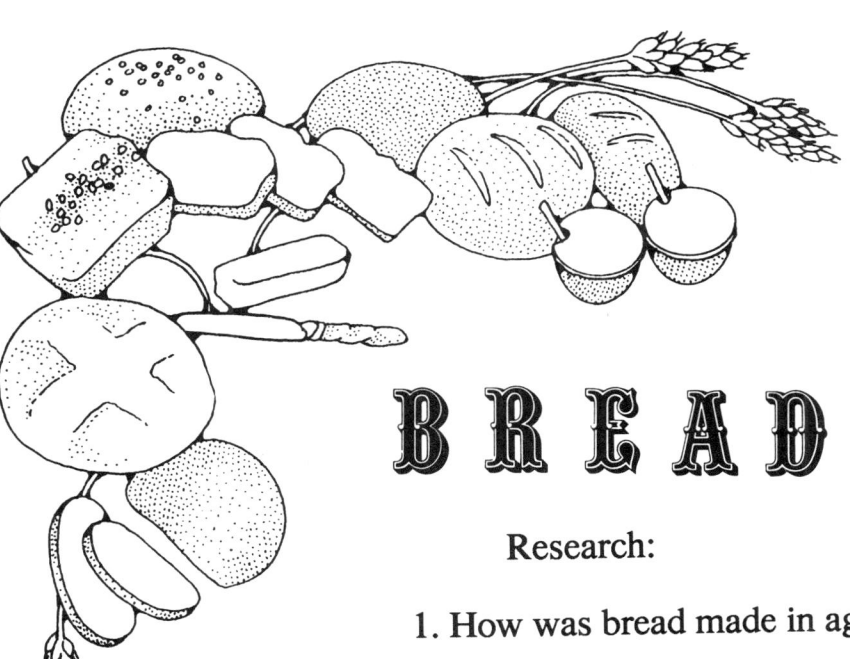
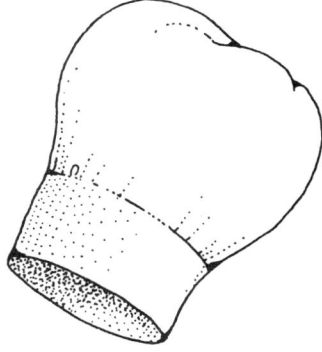

BREAD

Research:

1. How was bread made in ages past?

2. How does yeast work in dough?

3. How many kinds of bread are there?

4. Visit a bakery. What did you learn?

5. What is the nutritional value of different kinds of bread?

6. How many kinds of wheat are there?
   Where do they grow?
   How are they harvested?

7. Why is bread called *"the staff of life"*.

Further explorations:

1. *Give a demonstration on bread-making.*

2. *Develop a new bread recipe.*

MONEY

1. Coins of all countries: A report.

2. Early coins or units of exchange.

3. Coin collecting.

4. Visit a bank to determine what a a given unit of money is worth in all other major countries throughout the world.

5. How does money make money? Investigate this.

6. Antique coins:
   Where are they obtained?
   What are they worth?

7. Make a chart showing:
   <u>money unit</u>   <u>country</u>   <u>description</u>

8. Find out what this means,

   *"For a country's economy to be healthy,
   money must stay in motion."*

9. Who are "economists"?
   What service do they provide?

10. Make up a game in which money from three countries is used.

11. Design an investment game. Buy and sell items traditionally thought to be good investments: gold, gems, real estate, art works, and blue chip stocks.

Moneymaking Ways,

Means and

Schemes

1. List ways people of your age can earn money.

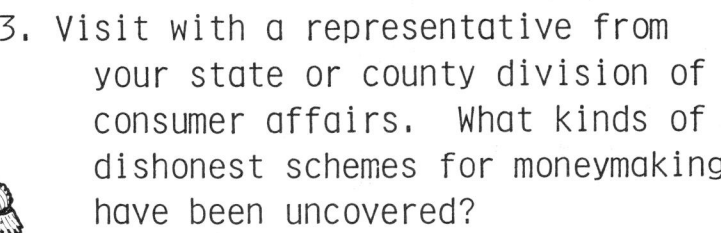

2. Plan a moneymaking idea. Test it. Did it work?

3. Visit with a representative from your state or county division of consumer affairs. What kinds of dishonest schemes for moneymaking have been uncovered?

4. Start a savings plan at your bank. Set up a record-keeping system for recording deposits and interest earned.

5. Interview your friends. How do they earn money?

6. Write a 20-year plan that outlines how much money you want to earn and the ways you will earn it.

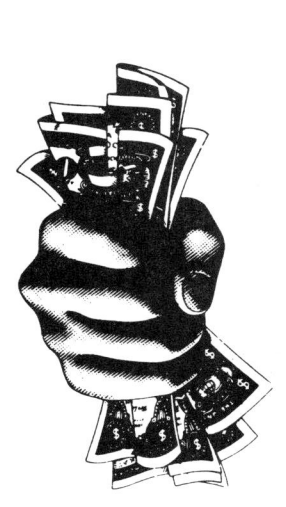

7. Visit with a banker, investment broker, or someone who is interested in investments. What are good investments at this time?

Form a musical group...

— and sing a song.

— and perform a song-and-dance routine.

— and play a concerto.

— and visit a recording studio.

— and cut a record.
"cutting a record" is making a record

— and design a dust jacket for your own original song.

— and write your own song.

— and volunteer to entertain a group of people.

— and impersonate a singing group.

— and teach others how to sing and play musical instruments.

— and form a music listening club.

— and make a set of puzzles based on musical singers and performers.

— and attend a concert.

ECONOMIC

NEWS

Today's information.

&

REPORTS

Fictitious accounts and folktales.

&

TALES

Information from books

and other sources.

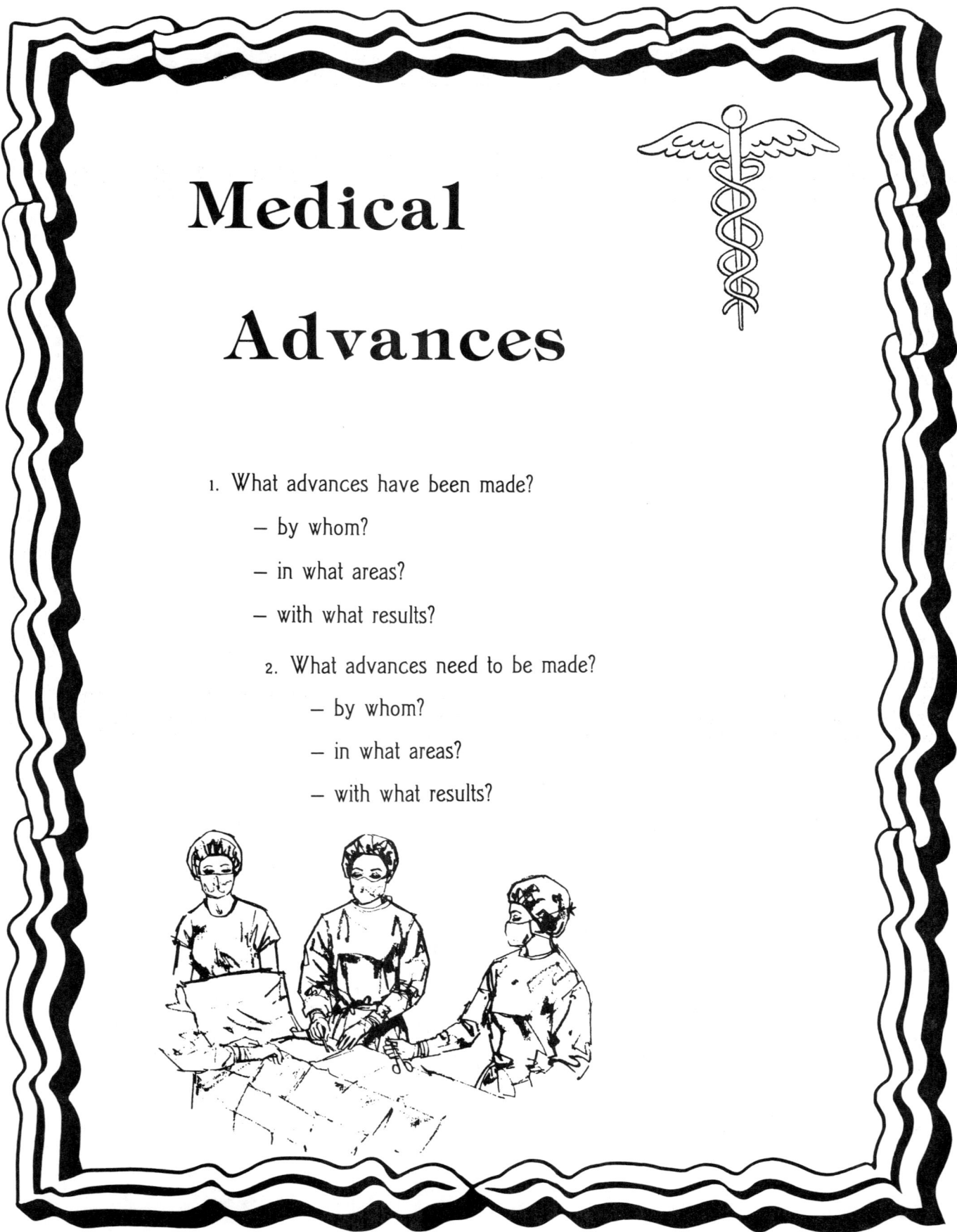

Medical

Advances

1. What advances have been made?

    – by whom?

    – in what areas?

    – with what results?

  2. What advances need to be made?

     – by whom?

     – in what areas?

     – with what results?

Make a poster

INFORMATION

A __poster__ should have a theme — one concept. All pictures and writings should be directly related to that theme or concept.

A POSTER should have:
1. one idea or concept.
2. a title to identify that theme, idea, or concept.
3. pictures and/or writing properly placed so that each item can be adequately seen or read.
4. some open-space border around all four sides so that the pictures/readings don't look "squeezed", or look like they are being forced off the poster.

Making a Work of Art Come Alive

Student Project: *To reproduce THE OLD BLIND GUITAR PLAYER and make the painting "come alive".*

(back row) Brian Fread Shauna Baker Stacey Foster
(front row) Laura Brannen Jason Doonan

Picasso's work was reproduced by the students on heavily-textured drapery fabric. They used a combination of pencil, markers, chalk, highlighters, fabric crayons, and oil crayons to reproduce the strong lines and multiple shades of blue and green.

Interpretation and story portrayed by students:

An old blind guitar player is sitting by himself — feeling sorry that he is blind. Some people walk by. They are planning a party. They comment on the sad guitar player.

"You'd be sad, too, if **you** were blind!" snaps the blind man.

The group gives another viewpoint:

"Ray Charles and Stevie Wonder are blind. And **they** don't sit around — moping and feeling sorry for themselves. They are singing — making themselves and others feel better."

The story ends with the whole group singing a song accompanied by the guitar player.

Making a Work of Art Come Alive

The OLD BLIND GUITAR PLAYER was painted by Pablo Picasso in 1903. This was during the "Blue Period" of the artist's life. THE OLD BLIND GUITAR PLAYER is painted predominately in blues and greens. The smooth, powerful lines depict a melancholy man who sees his blindness as an overwhelming handicap.

The Old Blind Guitar Player
painted by Pablo Picasso
(photocopy of it)

The Old Blind Guitar Player
reproduced by students

Student Project: To reproduce THE OLD BLIND GUITAR PLAYER and make the painting "come alive."

Any work of art may be reproduced and interpreted. This type of project encourages studying and interpreting works of art.

Student Projects - Ideas & Plans. © Leadership Publishers, 1994

Famous clowns....

Make-up techniques of clowns....

Influence of clowns ....

Types of clowns....

Body movements of clowns....

Purpose of clowns....

Clowns you've seen....

Creation of a clown's personality....

Uniqueness of each clown....

Clowns

Invent a . . .

new or better

HOTDOG

RUNNING SHOE

CALCULATOR

SHOESHINE EQUIPMENT

AIRPLANE

SEWING MACHINE

SAFETY PIN

TELEPHONE

MOUSETRAP

LIPSTICK

FABRIC

TISSUE

NOTEBOOK

SNOW REMOVER

ICE MELTER

UMBRELLA

SUN GLASSES

PAINT

RUGS

HAND WARMER

FOOT COOLER

MUSCLE MASSAGER

LIGHT BULB

CANDY

WATCH

BINOCULARS

TELEVISION SET

ABC....

Create an ABC book.

Create your book around a theme:

topic - your choice,

geographic area,

objects that rhyme,

things you like,

places you have been,

dreams you have,

....

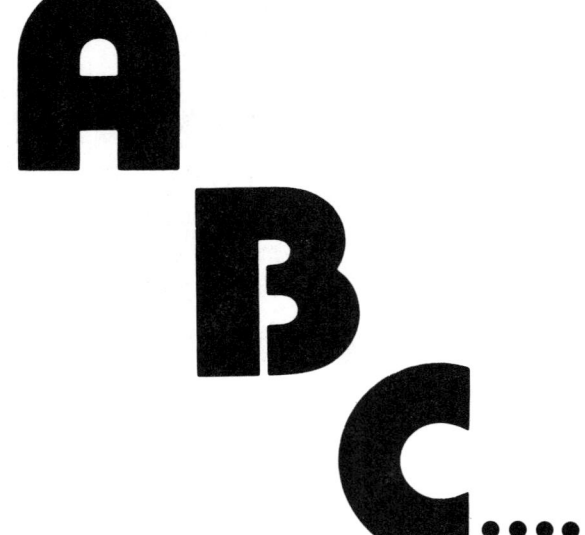

Architecture

Read about . . .
Classify . . .
Write a report on . . .
Interview someone who . . .
Compare one . . . to . . .
Hypothesize about . . .
Make a diorama of . . .
Take a field trip to . . .
Use a computer to . . .
Make a poster of . . .
Invent a . . .
Do a survey to find out . . .
Volunteer your services to . . .
Write a play . . .
Perform a play . . .
Write a song . . .
Sing a solo . . .
Form a musical group . . .
Collect oral history about . . .
Make a booklet of . . .
Draw a picture . . .
Collect . . .
Read poetry . . .
Write a poem . . .
Assemble a bibliography . . .
Write science fiction . . .
Write a fictional story . . .
Observe . . .
Experiment . . .
Write a letter to . . .
Redesign the . . .

ART

1. Visit an art gallery.

2. Study the works of one artist. Characterize that artist's style.

3. Make a matching puzzle: artists on one side and works of art on the other.

4. If you could own one original work of art, (and could afford it), which work of art would you purchase?

5. Make one of the works of art "come alive"- that is, continue the action suggested, or have the character(s) speak.

6. Art works are sometimes bought as a financial investment. Find out how art pieces can be a financial investment?

7. List 10 (or more) famous works of art. List where each is now located.

8. Consider within yourself, or ask an artist or photographer, "How does a portrait differ from a photograph?"

9. Make a dictionary of art tools and media. Assemble it into book form and put a copy in your school library.

10. Make a booklet of art prints. For each print:
    a. Describe the print, or
    b. Give your reaction to the print.

Student Projects - Ideas & Plans. © Leadership Publishers, 1994

HORSES

1. Classify horses into   groups.
   Describe the group and list horses within that group.

2. Read about raising and racing racehorses. Write a
   report on your findings.

3. Visit someone who has a horse used for recreational purposes.
   How much does it cost to have such a horse? What kind of
   care is required?   Other questions???

4. Horse racing is popular in many countries.
   List famous horse races and location of the race.

5. Explain the meaning of this quotation:

   "Horse racing is the sport of kings."

6. Read fictional stories about horses.

7. Write a story about a horse.

8. Complete this sentence:
   "If I could have any horse I
   wanted, I would have . . . "

9. Read about miniature horses.

10. Visit a state or other fair.
    What horses were exhibited?
    What "horse events" were
       featured?

Seafaring & Ocean

NEWS

Today's information.

REPORTS

Information from books and other sources.

TALES

Fictitious accounts and folktales.

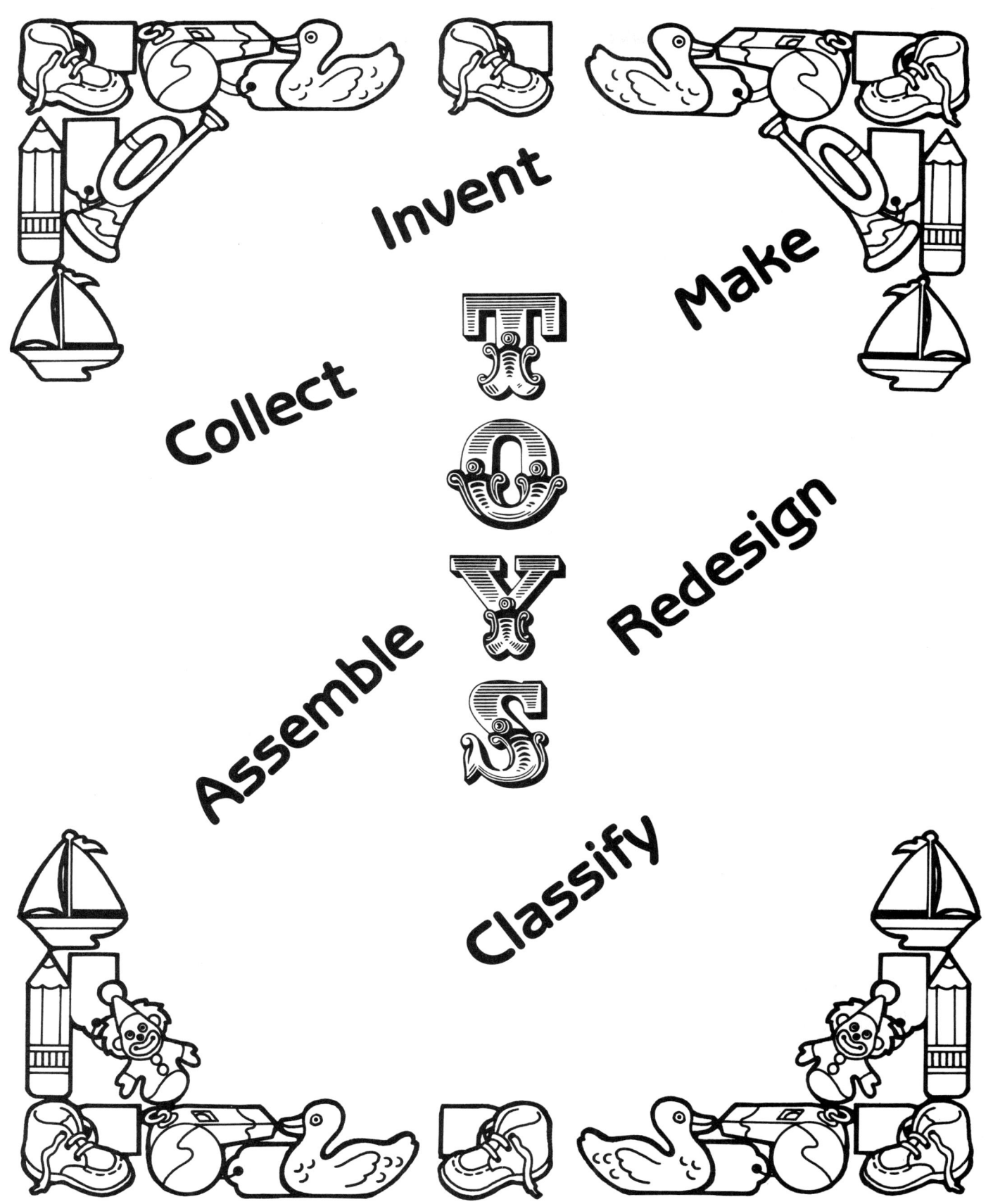

Invent

Make

Collect

Redesign

Assemble

Classify

Mayflower Compact

The MAYFLOWER COMPACT was the first self-governing agreement in America.

The MAYFLOWER COMPACT play, shared with readers on the following pages, is a humorous contemporary version of this important document.

To appreciate this contemporary edition, consult an encyclopedia to learn the actual terms of the original MAYFLOWER COMPACT signed by the Pilgrims in 1620.

Student authors: David Van Utrecht, Sara Lanphier, Brian Thomas, Ronnie Whitehead and Darcie Dop.

Authors: David   Sara   Brian   Ronnie   Darcie

CAST OF CHARACTERS
WRASLING BREWSTER, passenger on ship
REMEMBER ALLERTON, passenger on ship
HUMILITY COPER, passenger on ship
WILLIAM BRADFORD, passenger on ship
MOYSES FLETCHER, passenger on ship
JOHN RIGDALE, passenger on ship
DOROTHY BRADFORD, passenger, wife of William Bradford

SETTING: Mayflower ship as it rests in the harbor. 1620.

(Scene One: open stage)

WRASLING BREWSTER: (walks unto stage) I am Wrasling Brewster, son of William and Mary Brewster. I came over to America on the Mayflower. (steps to side)

WILLIAM BRADFORD: (enter, introduces self) I am William Bradford. My wife, Dorothy, and I were passengers on the Mayflower. I was later to become governor of Plymouth Colony. (steps to side)

MOYSES FLETCHER: (enters). Greetings. My name is Moyses Fletcher, a passenger on the Mayflower. The Mayflower was a three-masted sailing vessel of 180 tons.

JOHN RIGDALE: I, too, sailed on the Mayflower. The Mayflower was approximately 100 feet in length and 26 feet in width. This wasn't a lot of room for 100 people.

MOYSES FLETCHER: The Mayflower left the English port on September 16, 1620.

REMEMBER ALLERTON: (enters, introduces self) I am Remember Allerton, another member of the group that came on the Mayflower. My parents were Isaack and Mary Allerton.
   I was a good friend of Wrasling Brewster (looks at Wrasling and both smile). It was a good thing I had a friend on board ship because the trip was a long and difficult one.

JOHN RIGDALE: We had hot food only a few times. Most of the time we ate cold hard biscuits, cheese, and salted beef or fish.

HUMILITY COPER: (enters, introduces self) I am Humility Coper, another traveler on the Mayflower. I was the cousin of Edward and Ann Tillie.

Student Projects - Ideas & Plans. © Leadership Publishers, 1994

DOROTHY BRADFORD: I am William Bradford's wife, Dorothy Bradford.

We all tried to make our voyage comfortable. But many people got sick because we had no fresh fruit or vegetables. We were often cold. Some cold icy ocean water got into the boat.

HUMILITY COPER: William Butten died at sea. Oceanus Hopkins was born at sea. For 65 days we were tossed by the Atlantic Ocean.

WRASLING : While the MAYFLOWER lay at anchor off Massachusetts in November, 1620, several discontented members of the Pilgrim band had talked of mutiny.

REMEMBER: To calm them, their leaders agreed to prepare a written document. The Mayflower Compact, as this document was later to be called, expressed the idea that everyone would have fair treatment.

MOYSES FLETCHER: A government would be set up to rule the colony.

HUMILITY: Forty-one men signed the compact in the ship's cabin.

WILLIAM BRADFORD: We agreed to obey the laws that we would pass.

WRASLING: The Mayflower Compact was an important step along the road to self government in the New World.

DOROTHY BRADFORD: The Mayflower Compact contained only 150 words. The last 41 words contained the actual agreement terms. William Bradford will read you these last 41 words:

WILLIAM BRADFORD: (reads) "We shall enact, constitute and frame just and equal laws, ordinances, acts and constitutions and offices, from time to time, as shall be thought most necessary for the general good of the colony. All who sign, promise to obey these laws."

(All bow to audience . Wrasling and William leave. Humility and Dorothy step to one side of the stage. John and Moyses step to the other. . REMEMBER, starts to leave but then returns)

REMEMBER: We forget to tell you some information. I'll tell you now. This information is not as well-known as the information we just told you. (pause, take a step)

Before we signed that agreement, the adults were arguing about some issues.

(REMEMBER steps to the side and scene goes to one side of stage, where Rigdale and Fletcher are arguing).

Scene Two: RIGDALE and FLETCHER

JOHN RIGDALE: It won't work!

MOYSES FLETCHER: It will too. We got to do it.

JOHN RIGDALE: Only an idiot would think that plan would work.

MOYSES FLETCHER: You said it, not me.

WILLIAM BRADFORD: (enters) What's the problem here?

JOHN RIGDALE: This fool, Moyses Fletcher, thinks we can make an agreement that will make life in our new colony easier and happier.

WILLIAM BRADFORD: That sounds like a good idea. So, what's the problem?

JOHN RIGDALE: Go ahead, Fletcher. Tell him what you want in the agreement.

MOYSES FLETCHER: The agreement should make sure each person gets:
   1. Pizza every Tuesday
   2. Free video game tokens for everyone over three years old.
   3. Each person will be entitled to 30 minutes in the private bathroom.
   4. Nobody has to eat vegetables.

RIGDALE: I still don't think it will work. I won't agree to some of those terms.

FLETCHER: Then, what will you agree to?

(RIGDALE and FLETCHER walk off while REMEMBER continues.)

REMEMBER: And that was just one of the problems. Another problem came when they were ready to sign it. Some men couldn't read or write.

There were other problems. One of those problems concerned the women. The women were angry because their signatures weren't required. (fade out)

Scene Three:: HUMILITY COPER and DOROTHY BRADFORD.

HUMILITY: I hear the men signed today. I hope they have fun keeping that agreement.

DOROTHY: Yes, they signed the agreement today.

HUMILITY: Since we women didn't sign it, we don't have to keep it.

DOROTHY: Now, Humility. It is up to our menfolk to tell us what to think.

HUMILITY: As long as I didn't sign it, I don't have to keep it.

DOROTHY: But, Humility, my dear. You are overreacting. We will not survive unless we agree.

HUMILITY: I'll never agree. My Mother should have called me DETERMINED instead of HUMILITY.

DOROTHY: You are so young. You must learn a very important lesson.

HUMILITY: If that lesson means letting men do the signing, and women do the doing, then I'm not interested in the lesson.

DOROTHY: The trick to happy living is to let men THINK they make all the decisions.

(scene fades out)

REMEMBER: After many compromises, the final version of the Mayflower Compact contained these provisions (all players enter):

REMEMBER: Pizza every Tuesday

WRASLING: Hamburgers, with lots of catsup and optional onion rings, served rare, medium, and well done, every other day.

BRADFORD: Free video game tokens for everyone over three years of age.

HUMILITY: Each person is entitled to 30 minutes in the private bathroom. If one goes overtime one day, the offending time will be subtracted from the next day's allotment.

DOROTHY: Everybody has to eat vegetables.

MOYSES: There shall be no established bedtime for children. Parents must be asleep by 8:30, 9:30 on weekends.

JOHN RIGDALE: All laws that are passed shall be followed.

WRASLING: All laws shall be for the common good of the colony.

DOROTHY: All laws shall be just and fair to men, women, and children.

MOYSES: Parties can last three days, and three days only.

REMEMBER: School sessions will be from 12:00- 1:00 on Monday through Wednesday.

HUMILITY: Schools must provide quality lunches and adequate recess time and equipment.

JOHN RIGDALE: The governor of the colony will be elected by secret ballot by everyone over 15 years of age.

WILLIAM BRADFORD: And so the compact, signed by everyone, came to be known as:

ALL: THE COLONY'S COMIC COMPACT.

Student Projects - Ideas & Plans. © Leadership Publishers,1994

Spotlight
Your
Cultural, Ethnic,
and
Geographic Heritage

Interview someone who . . .

has won a contest.

is a published author.

played professional sports.

is your neighbor.

is a research scientist.

takes care of sick people.

is kind-hearted to many people.

raises dogs or cats.

likes cheese on apple pie.

is on the "A" honor roll at school.

is principal at your school.

served some time in the military service.

Collect oral history about. . .

1. *Relatives who live in different places.*

2. *Older brothers, sisters, aunts, relatives.*

3. *Business and industry located in your area.*

4. *An elderly neighbor or friend.*

5. *Someone who fought in a war.*

6. *Someone who was or is well-known (famous).*

7. *Survivors of a natural disaster.*

8. *Immigrants who immigrated to escape some form of persecution or slavery.*

Museum Plan

Directions: Design a museum. List contents. Add pictures to your descriptions.

Purpose of the museum (history, culture, music ....)

_____

Contents of the Museum - include pictures:

Student Projects - Ideas & Plans. © Leadership Publishers,1994

Space Travel

Directions:
Add *your own ideas (words or pictures) to complete this sketch.*

OCCUPATIONS

Read about. . .
Classify. . .
Write a report on. . .
Interview someone who. . .
Compare one. . . to. . .
Hypothesize about. . .
Make a diorama of. . .
Take a field trip to. . .
Use a computer to. . .
Make a poster of. . .
Invent a. . .
Do a survey to find out. . .
Volunteer your services to. . .

Write a play. . .
Perform a play. . .
Write a song. . .
Sing a solo. . .
Form a musical group. . .
Collect oral history about. . .
Make a booklet of. . .
Draw a picture. . .
Collect. . .
Read poetry. . .
Write a poem. . .
Assemble a bibliography. . .
Write science fiction. . .
Write a fictional story. . .

Observe. . .
Experiment. . .
Write a letter to. . .
Redesign the. . .
Interpret. . .
Translate. . .
. . .other. . .

UFOs

What?

Description?

Where?

Seen by Whom?

(U) Unidentified

(F) Flying

(O) Objects

```
▲▲▲▲▲▲▲▲▲▲▲▲▲▲▲▲▲▲▲▲▲▲▲▲▲▲▲▲▲▲▲▲▲▲▲▲▲▲▲▲▲▲
```
INFORMATION BOX

*A diorama is a three-dimensional representation.
A diorama shows back ground, figures, and objects related
to the content depicted.*

```
▲▲▲▲▲▲▲▲▲▲▲▲▲▲▲▲▲▲▲▲▲▲▲▲▲▲▲▲▲▲▲▲▲▲▲▲▲▲▲▲▲▲
```

Make a diorama of . . .

1. an historical event.

2. a chapter of a book.

3. an event from someone's life.

4. a memory.

5. an athletic event.

6. a military encounter.

7. a school scene.

8. a day in the life of someone - a pioneer, farmer, mother ... .

9. a scientist working in a laboratory.

10. the history of your family.

11. the history of - your county, state, province, or country....

12. a Shakespearean play.

13. a weather event - flood, hurricane.... .

14. a career - show duties related to it.

15. the steps in completing a product or project.

Student Projects - Ideas & Plans. © Leadership Publishers,1994

1. *What are they?*

2. *How are they formed?*

3. *Describe their:*

   > *beauty...*
   >
   > *power...*
   >
   > *danger...*
   >
   > *advantage...*
   >
   > *disadvantage...*
   >
   > *softness...*
   >
   > *movements...*

4. *Make a collection of paper snowflakes.*

SNOW FLAKES

Student Projects - Ideas & Plans. © Leadership Publishers, 1994

ANTIQUES

1. *When is something classified as an antique?*

2. *Visit an antique shop. Report your observations.*

3. *Which antiques are considered most valuable?*

4. *Do you own an antique? Report on it.*

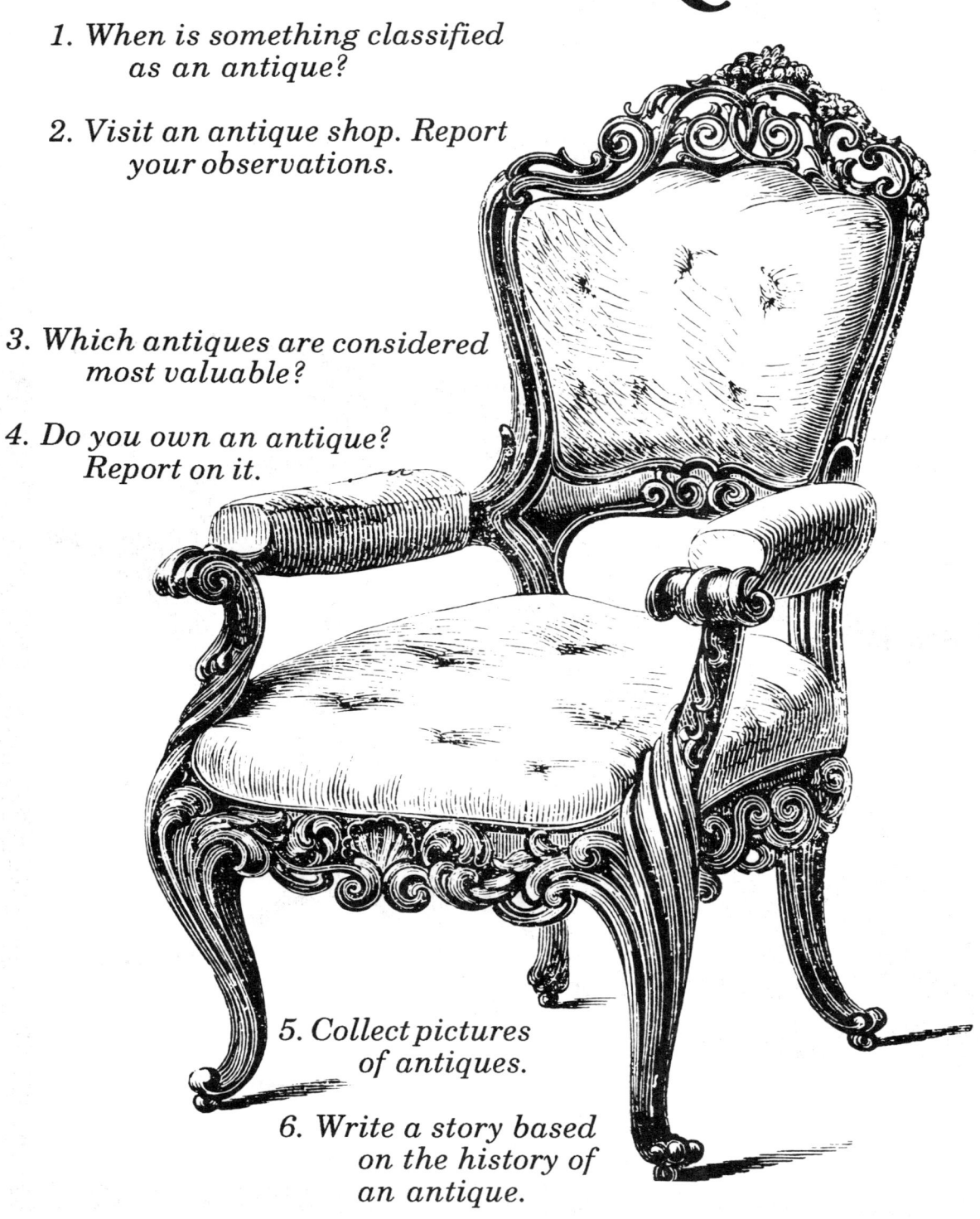

5. *Collect pictures of antiques.*

6. *Write a story based on the history of an antique.*

Fingerprints

1. What are fingerprints?
2. How are fingerprints recorded?
3. When were fingerprints first used?
4. How are fingerprints classified?
5. Record your own fingerprints.
6. Write a story in which fingerprints are important.

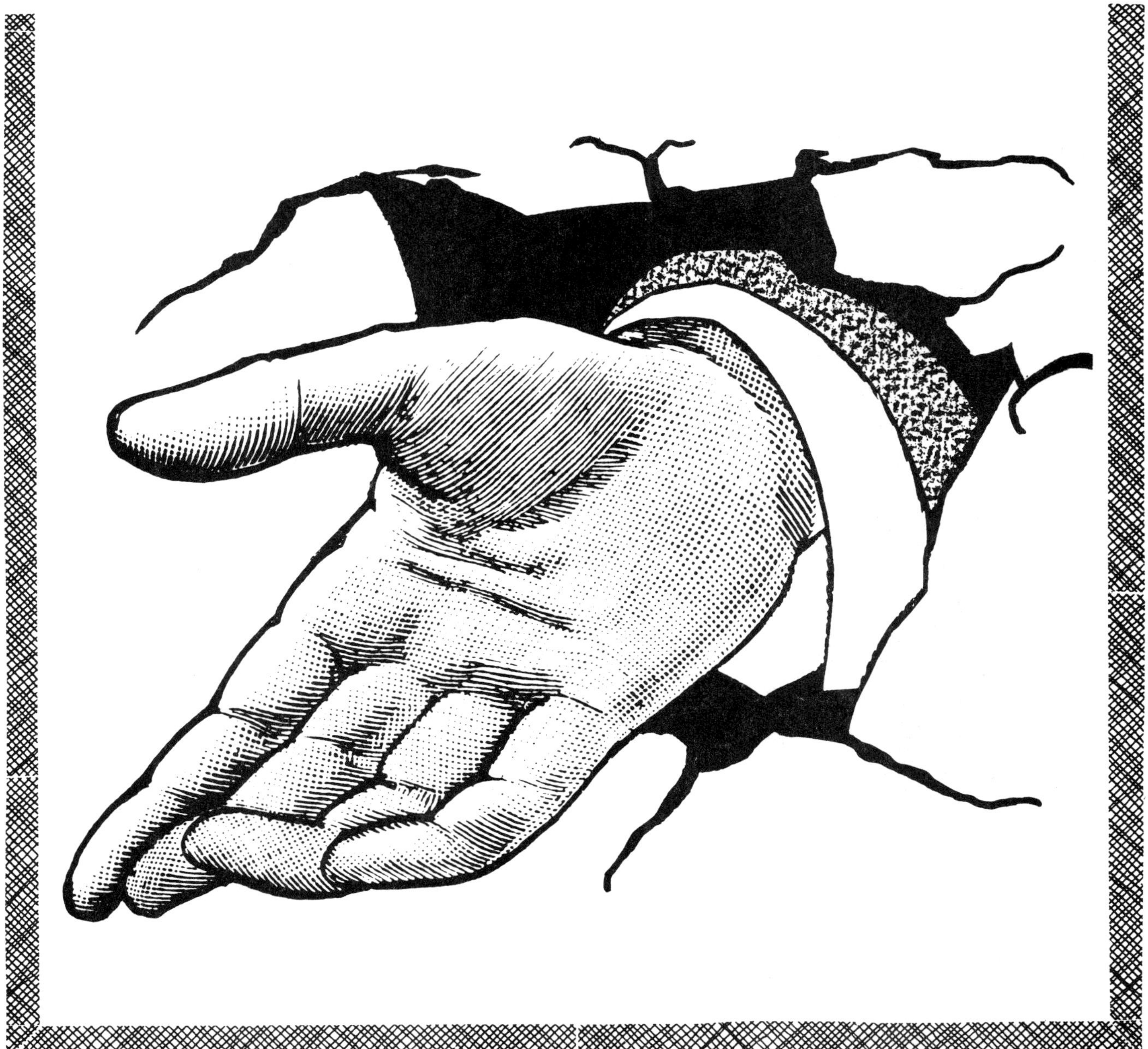

dreams

1. What are dreams?

2. Why are some dreams all right and others are nightmares?

3. Read about dreams.

4. Think about dreams and how dreams help us solve problems.

5. List some theories about the origins and meanings of dreams.

TELEPHONES

1. Make a timeline tracing major achievements in telephone communications.

2. Learn how computer phone modems work.

3. List ways in which the telephone could be improved.

4. List inventors who contributed to the invention and/or improvement of the telephone.

5. Telephones are shaped in many ways. Design several that would reflect your interest and style.

6. Research: How do cordless telephones work?

DXNARD the WARRIOR

and the Mystical Ring of Truth

by

Martin   Geurts

Author is currently in 8th grade. This fantasy story was written when Martin was in 7th grade.

As the warrior rode his kanghorse through the dense forest, near the enchanted city of Pentagarn, he noticed the Heboggs, a ruthless gang, known for their use of sorcery to deform and disintegrate men and children alike.

"What brings you to the forest, Dxnard The Conquerer?" asked Leechler, the leader of the Heboggs. "Don't tell me you came to ruin our fun."

And with that the leader of the Heboggs rapped his cloak tightly about himself, and chanted the invisibility spell and vanished!

"You can't hide from me, "cried Dxnard The Conquerer. And he pulled the spearshot, a small devise that fires dart-like spears about 5 inches long, from his cloak. Dxnard strapped the spearshot to his hand, and leaped onto the tree limb about six feet above his head. Then he bent his wrist so that the spearshot was pointing at the fruit of the bimm tree. (The fruit from the bimm tree has a powdery substance in it used in making red acid dye).

"Aaye!" cried Leechler, wiping the powdery acid substance from his eyes. "Attack!"

And at this the Heboggs started preparing spells!

"This'll give me a chance to use my triple bolo!" cried Dxnard the Conquerer, flinging the special bolo at the Heboggs. As the ball-weighted strings flew through the air, one of the Heboggs' spells disintegrated the bolo. At the sight of this, knowing the Heboggs could only recite one spell a day apiece, Dxnard picked the first spell user for his slingbow, the slingshot type weapon that hooked over the fingers and fires arrows that are 7-8 inches long. He fired, taking careful aim not to hit the Hebogg. Just as the arrow was launched, another spell was cast and the arrow turned to stone and immediately fell to the ground.

"I'm going to have to get behind them, or else my weapons won't work," Dxnard said to himself. "And I know just how I'm going to do it!"

Taking the Helmet of Invisibility out of his weapons pack, he placed the helmet on his head and vanished. Then he reappeared behind the Heboggs!

"Come out and fight like a warrior, "dared the Heboggs. "Let us have a little fun, Dxnard."

Taking great care not to make a sound, Dxnard took out his favorite weapon, the trapnet, a steel-like mesh that can only be cut by the Dagger of Hades and the Sword of the Golden Leopard - the sword that Dxnard himself carries. Then, still relying on surprise, Dxnard threw the net upon them, causing them to be captured!

Student Projects - Ideas & Plans. © Leadership Publishers,1994

"Now that you are, shall we say, 'under wraps', I shall call the royal guard." Dxnard replied, and blew in his horn. The royal guards immediately appeared and took the Heboggs into custody.

"Now, I shall get back to my engagement with my friend, Tomox the Wizard, to see what magical weapons he has for me, " Dxnard said to himself.

Then he hopped onto his kanghorse and rode towards the enchanted city of Pentagarn, where the wizard lives.

"Tomox, " called Dxnard, "what do you have for me this time?"

"A quest, and a few mystical weapons, " replied Tomox."Enter."

As Dxnard entered the workshop of the fabled wizard Tomox, he felt the tingling sensation he usually felt when he entered the magical place.

Entering the secret room, where the two discussed quests Dxnard spotted the wizard. He sat down in a cushioned, wooden chair.

"What are my weapons and what do they do?" Dxnard asked earnestly. "And what is my quest?"

"First of all, your quest is to return the Mystical Ring of Truth to the Forbidden Mountain. The Ring was stolen by Ceaser the Invincible for his museum.

"And as for your weapons," replied Tomox. "They are simple but effectively lethal. The first and most dangerous is the Daggerrang, a boomerang-type weapon that has a razor-sharp blade that can wound or even kill an enemy with one toss. And it always comes back to its thrower, with sometimes fatal outcomes - if not caught correctly.

"The second weapon is the Iron Whip, usually referred to as the Iron Cobra. It can be used as a whip. It delivers a powerful sting that can knock out nearly any enemy. Or it can be used as a rope that can wrap itself around any wood or metal.

" And last but not least, is the weapon called Whiplash, which is a mystical ball-and-chain type weapon attached to a sturdy pole by a heavy steel chain. Metal spikes jut out of the ball. This weapon has been known to break a hole in 6-inch thick dobalt, the strongest substance in the universe!"

"These weapons are truly fabulous, and I will use them wisely," replied Dxnard.

"You have only 3 earth days to return the ring to its proper place before evil conquers all."

And with that, the wizard wrapped his cloak about himself and chanted a spell that teleported him near the location of the Mystical Ring of truth.

As Dxnard unknowingly scanned the rugged terrain, a Mountain Vapor, one of the deadliest animals in the Desert of Mountains where Dxnard was teleported, sprang from a cliff 40 foot up, and landed on Dxnard, causing them both to fall into a ravine 1,300 ft. deep!

Thinking that the only way to save himself and the Mountain Vapor, Dxnard unraveled the Iron Cobra. Holding on to one end Dxnard threw the Iron Cobra upwards. Fortunately, it wrapped around a thick branch jutting out of the ravine's wall. Now Dxnard could swing across the ravine, just in time to grab ahold of the Mountain Vapor's tail just before they swung into a cave on the other side of the crevasse!

Becoming fast friends, because of Dxnard's daring feat, the two made their way down the dark corridor.

Sensing danger, the Mountain Vapor emitted a low growl, meaning slight danger.

Student Projects - Ideas & Plans. © Leadership Publishers,1994

Taking extreme caution, the two silently made their way around the turn in the walkway. Finding no danger, the two entered a large museum-type room, with every type of weapon, animal, and even some wax statues of the greatest warriors that ever lived, including one of Dxnard himself!

"Who dares to enter the Museum of Ceaser?" cried a six-foot-eight, very muscular man armed with a triple crossbow, a helmet, a shield, a fighting staff, and a sword with the inscription 'Invincible'!

"I, Dxnard the Warrior, dares, " cried Dxnard, jumping onto a near-by table. "And I have come for the Mystical Ring of Truth so that this lovely planet will not be conquered by evil scum like you!"

"Ahh, but you are mistaken, Dxnard the Warrior," replied Ceaser. "For evil scum like me will destroy this lovely planet, including you, unless you and your pet can find the ring. The ring is somewhere in this mountain. You and your pet must defeat me and my 30 greatest warriors which I trained myself. Or you will meet your doom."

And with that, Ceaser jumped 30 ft. into the air and landed on a platform, which was connected to a door. The door opened and Ceaser disappeared!

"Well my friend, it seems that we have our work cut out for ourselves, "replied Dxnard. "And we had best start our new quest immediately."

As the two set off, the mountain vapor, which Dxnard nicknamed Panthro, was guiding Dxnard (with its senses) towards a heavy metal door held tightly closed by a thick band of steel-type leather. Taking out the Sword of the Golden Leapord, Dxnard slashed off the band and swung the door inward, and discovered a low ceiling, dark corridor. He walked onward, Panthro leading the way.

"Panthro, what's wrong?" Dxnard asked when Panthro suddenly stopped and started sniffing the air. "Is there danger ahead?"

As soon as these words were uttered, a large Hoboglin jumped out of the shadows, armed with a sword, a full coat of armor, a shield, dagger, spear, a spiked club and a crossbow!

"Dxnard, I have come to destroy you", cried the Hobogoblin. "Because you are a threat to my master's existence. So I must kill you."

And with that the Hoboglin raised his crossbow and fired a poisoned arrow at Dxnard!

Easily dogging the arrow, Dxnard took out the Dangerrang and tossed at the Hoboglins neck!

Ducking, the Hoboglin took out his spiked club, and lunged at Dxnard!

"A foolish mistake young warrior," Dxnard laughed. "Panthro, attack!" And with that the huge cat lunged at the young foe, causing the Hoboglin to faint from fear!

After reviving the young lad Dxnard learns why and how the young lad became a warrior.

"When I was young my family was taken hostage by a warrior who had a shield, with the name DXNARD inscribed on it." recalled the Hoboglin. "Several days passed. Then a man who said that he wished to destroy a man named Dxnard the Conquer, asked if Dxnard had passed by. Hearing this, I told him my story, and begged to go along with him. He trained me, and after several years of training he added me to his band of warriors as a spy. Later I found out that what he was doing was evil, but I was destined to destroy you, Dxnard for what you did to my family!

"That is a very touching story young friend, but it was not me, I swear," Dxnard replied. "For I was only a young man when that tragedy occurred. My guess is that it was your adopted father Ceaser."

"But why would Ceaser do a thing like that?" questioned the hogoblin. "For he has been like a father to me."

"My guess is that he wanted to use your anger as a weapon against me, "Dxnard replied."By the way, would you like to help me find the ring? I'm absolutely sure you could help me find it. And besides, what is one more companion?"

"I would be honored to accompany you, Dxnard," replied the hogobloin. "And besides I think I know where the ring is!"

"Where is it?" asked Dxnard.

"Every day Ceaser goes into a gigantic vault to check on something that must be very important. There are 14 or 15 guards there at all times," said Samson, the young hogoblin. "And besides the vault's walls are 8 ft.thick!"

"That vault wall could prove to be a problem," Dxnard remarked. "Where is this vault?"

"Deep in this mountain,"said Samson. "Follow me!"

And with that the young hogoblin raced down the narrow winding passage. After several minutes Samson came to and abrupt halt.

"Shh."whispered Samson, "some of the guards are eating at their posts. And look at their weapons!"

Sure enough the guards were heavily armed with swords, daggers, crossbows, spears, and various other weapons, and it looked like they knew how to use them too!

"Why do they wear different colored tunics?" asked Dxnard wanting to know everything about his opponents." I see that most of them are wearing black or purple."

"The lighter the color the better the fighter," replied Samson. "As you have probably figured out because of my purple tunic.

"Sounds like we will meet doom unless a plan comes to my mind," Dxnard replied and sat there for a few minutes his eyes closed, and his head resting on the palm of his hand. Obviously a plan was forming in his mind.

Minutes later.....

"I have it, "cried Dxnard, "I have it. And with that he told Samson and Panthro his plan.

Taking great care not to arouse suspicion, Samson went into a nearby supply closet and picked out a purple hooded tunic for Dxnard and a large chain for Pantrho, to make it seem that Dxnard had captured the deadly beast. As soon as Dxnard and Panthro donned their disguises, the trio entered the nearby recreation facility, used to develop the skills of the warriors of Ceaser.

"Look what I, Leo the Leathel have captured," said Dxnard disguising his voice. "A Mountain Vapor!"

"You lie you little worm. Somehow you have created an illusion of a Mountain Vapor," challenged the warriors. "He lies. Let us have him let the creature loose and see how real this so-called Mountain Vapor really is!"

"You asked for it," replied Dxnard. "Panthro attack!" And with that the huge cat leaped forward, clawing and scratching, killing the enemy with its lethal claws!

As soon as Panthro killed the six or seven purple-clad figures, the three looked over their few measly, scratch-like wounds. They saw a strange, mysterious looking passage. Making no sound, the trio entered the weird tunnel, and followed it until it came to a large statue of Ceaser. Noticing all of the footprints leading up to the statue, the three decided that this must be a secret passage that leads to the vault, where the ring is hidden.

As the three searched around for a secret lever or button to open the door-like statue, they did not notice the white clad figure approaching them from above with an arrow aimed at Dxnard's heart!

Feeling the presence of another person besides his friends, Dxnard naturally looked up. Just in time to see the arrow streaking towards his own chest! Taking out his daggerrang, and taking perfect aim, Dxnard threw it and prayed for one, just one, lucky break.

Meanwhile, Dxnard's two companions found the switch, and the secret panel and continued down the torch-lighted tunnel. Hearing sound around the corner up ahead, the two quietly edged their way around the corner and spotted a vault 10 ft. tall and had 15 white-clad guards surrounding it!

"We must tell Dxnard of our discovery," whispered Samson. "We must!"

"What are you doing here you purple clad peasant?" said a voice behind them. "Show me your admittance card, or be terminated!"

As the two allies of Dxnard were being put under the "third degree" Dxnard saw the deadly arrow split in half, right before his very eyes! Reaching up with his right hand Dxnard expertly caught the daggerrang. All of a sudden, Dxnard heard a sickening thud and saw the attacker laying on the floor with his head cut off. The daggerang, after spitting the arrow evidently had enough momentum going that it hit the attacker in the neck, causing him and his separated head to fall to the ground!

Noticing that his two companions were nowhere to be seen, Dxnard took a look at the statue. Noticing a piece of bright purple material, taking a step forward as to get a closer look, Dxnard slipped and instinctively grabbed at the nearest thing, the statues arm. Almost instantly the figure slid counter-clock wise on a well concealed track, causing Dxnard to plunge into the tunnel. He was knocked unconscious!

Minutes later Dxnard came to, dusted himself off, and realized he needed rest and a warm meal. Dxnard took out the cooking stone, a rock that if hit on the top with the other half, actually can be hot enough to cook a meal for 1 to 5 people. Then he took out some emergency rations and a bed roll. After eating only what he needed, Dxnard put the rest in two little containers for Samson and Panthro, and dozed of to sleep, only to awake minutes later, refreshed and ready for action by a war cry! Before he went to sleep, Dxnard had the Iron Cobra laying near by!

Dodging the oncomer's spear, Dxnard snapped the Iron Cobra at the figure, knocking the attacker unconscious!

When the figure finally came to, Dxnard was there, ready to attack the the attacker if he didn't talk, or if he tried to escape.

"Talk, you lowlife, or you will talk to the Whipplash, my mystical ball and chain!" threatened Dxnard. "Talk!"

To preserve his hide from certain injury, the figure talked, telling where Samson and Panthro were being held captive, and where the guards were stationed, even the safe's combination! (little did Dxnard know that everything that the figure told him was exactly opposite of how it really was!)

"If the information that you have given me is faulty, you worm, we shall meet again," threatened Dxnard as he tied up his prisoner. "And it won't be so pleasant for you."

As Dxnard walked down the passage, he thought of how easily the figure told him what he needed to know.

Student Projects - Ideas & Plans. © Leadership Publishers, 1994

"I will just do everything exactly opposite of how he told me," Dxnard thought."Exactly opposite."

While Dxnard was reversing his directions, his companions were in a small, dark room with guards hidden in the shadows on tiny platforms on the every wall, including two above the door ready to spring into action if the door should open!

Hours passed and Dxnard had still not made an attempt to rescue the two, or so it seemed, but Dxnard had to wait 1 hour to act after the guards were taken food. One hour.

Unknown to the cook, Dxnard slipped some of the Tomox's sleeping powder into the meals for the guards while he was getting the spices. (It takes 1 hour for the powder to enter the blood stream of hoboglins.)

"The potion shall go into effect." Dxnard started the countdown," 5,4,3,2,1,now!"

Waiting a couple of minutes to make sure that the powder worked, Dxnard went to where the food was delivered. He slowly opened the door. Taking no chances of an ambush, Dxnard took a flying leap into the air, landed and somersaulted and stood up under the platform opposite the door. He looked around the room and saw his companions to the left of him, above him on every wall were the sleeping guards, and to the right was a passage.

Going to his companions, Dxnard loosed their bonds and fed them with the food in the little containers, and told them why he didn't come sooner. Minutes later, the trio was at the other side of the room, and they continued down the passage. As they walked, the passage came to a halt at the base of a ladder, which they climbed up. Opening the trap-door above his head, Dxnard climbed out into a large vault. And in the center upon a high pedestal was the Mystical Ring of Truth!

Taking great care Dxnard lifted Samson onto his back. As Samson lifted down the ring, purple clad guards rushed in to protect the ring from Dxnard. Panthro made short work of them. With the ring in hand, Dxnard wished for a portal, which arrived via the ring, and Dxnard was teleported to the Mystical mountains (with his friends of course), and then to Tomox's place for a short celebration for they had escaped from Ceaser, and saved the planet, or had they?

The End.

GLOSSARY of TERMS for DXNARD

BIMM TREE: rare tree that only grows near enchanted cities; fruit contains acid-like powder used in making dye.

DAGGER OF HADES: a special dagger whose origin is unknown; can cut any substance.

DAGGERANG: boomerang -type weapon that has a razor sharp blade used to inflict wounds on an enemy; always comes back to thrower.

DESERT OF MOUNTAINS: dry barren place consisting mainly of mountains.

DOBALT: steel-type material; can withstand 20000 lbs. of pressure; strongest substance in the universe.

SLINGBOW: slingshot-type weapon that slips over the fingers and fires small arrows, 7-8 inches long.

SPEARSHOT: a small device that fires five-inch dart-like spears.

SWORD OF THE GOLDEN LEOPARD: Dxnard's sword, golden blade with the inscription "forever".

TRIPLE BOLO: nine ball-weighted strings used to entangle or slow down the enemy.

TRAPNET: steel-type net not cuttable except by the Dagger of Hades or the Sword of the Golden Leopard.

WHIPLASH: mystical ball and chain.

FIGHTING STAFF: sturdy pole used to inflict wounds.

HELMET OF INVISIBILITY: mystical weapon that when placed on the head causes the wearer to become invisible.

HEBOGGS: ruthless gang of mutants who use their magic for evil.

HOGAR: small elf-like creature

IRON COBRA: a whip -type weapon that delivers a powerful sting that causes loss of consciousness, or it can wrap around nearly every substance.

IRON WHIP: see Iron Cobra

"INVINCIBLE": inscription on Ceaser's sword that means "not able to be defeated".

KANGHORSE: part kangaroo part horse used as a means of transportation

MOUNTAIN VAPOR: cat-like animal that lives only in the Desert of Mountains.

MUSEUM OF CEASER: where Ceaser admires his treasures, and lives.

MYSTICAL RING OF TRUTH: source of all of the planet's power; if removed, planet will be destroyed.

PANTHRO: see Mountain Vapor

SHIELD: device used to block weapons

END.

Person I think is interesting:

who?

why?

... some facts about ....

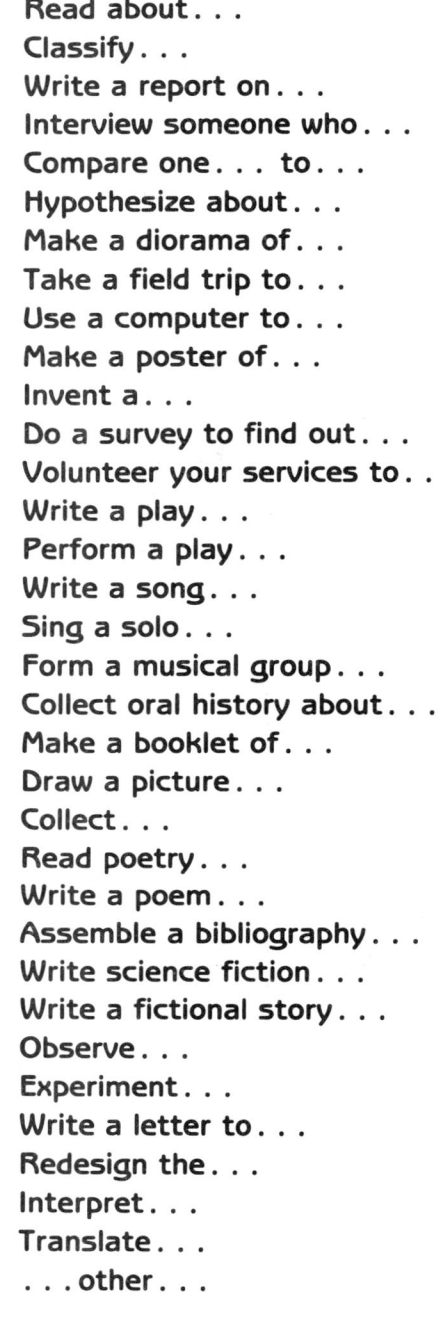

Read about . . .
Classify . . .
Write a report on . . .
Interview someone who . . .
Compare one . . . to . . .
Hypothesize about . . .
Make a diorama of . . .
Take a field trip to . . .
Use a computer to . . .
Make a poster of . . .
Invent a . . .
Do a survey to find out . . .
Volunteer your services to . . .
Write a play . . .
Perform a play . . .
Write a song . . .
Sing a solo . . .
Form a musical group . . .
Collect oral history about . . .
Make a booklet of . . .
Draw a picture . . .
Collect . . .
Read poetry . . .
Write a poem . . .
Assemble a bibliography . . .
Write science fiction . . .
Write a fictional story . . .
Observe . . .
Experiment . . .
Write a letter to . . .
Redesign the . . .
Interpret . . .
Translate . . .
. . . other . . .

Make a Collage

Sample Collage

A <u>collage</u> is a display made by pasting various clippings and objects onto a surface. All objects and clippings are part of a main theme.

Compare one... to...

part of the country . . . . another part of the country

FORM OF EXERCISE . . . . . ANOTHER FORM OF EXERCISE

toothpaste. . . . . another brand of toothpaste

BRAND OF TENNIS SHOE . . . . ANOTHER BRAND OF TENNIS SHOE

cola soft drink . . . . . . another cola soft drink

MYSTERY WRITER' STORIES . . ANOTHER MYSTERY WRITER'S STORIES

nail polish . . . . another nail polish

COMPUTER . . . . .ANOTHER COMPUTER

word processing system. . . another word processing
system

DONUT . . . . ANOTHER DONUT

radio . . . . another radio

Sample comparison:

COMPARISON		BRANDS OF ICE CREAM	N-3
	COST/GALLON	NUMBER OF FLAVORS	TASTE●
BRAND X	$3.49	18	1
BRAND Y	$1.79	4	4
BRAND Z	$5.25	11	2

● TASTE CODE
1 - EXCELLENT
2 - ALL RIGHT
3 - AVERAGE
4 - UNINTERESTING
5 - DULL
6 - AWFUL

Recreational   Activities

identify...
describe...   **Related to Ice**
classify...
read about...
report on...
demonstrate "how to"...
observe...
interview someone who...
report about...
make a poster of...
write adventurous account of. .
Write and perform a play related to ice.
Invent a new ice-related activity.
Invent a new technique for ice-fishing.
Read "Hans Brinker and the Silver
        Skates" and other ice-related stories.
Describe the life of the fish below
        the icy surface of the water.

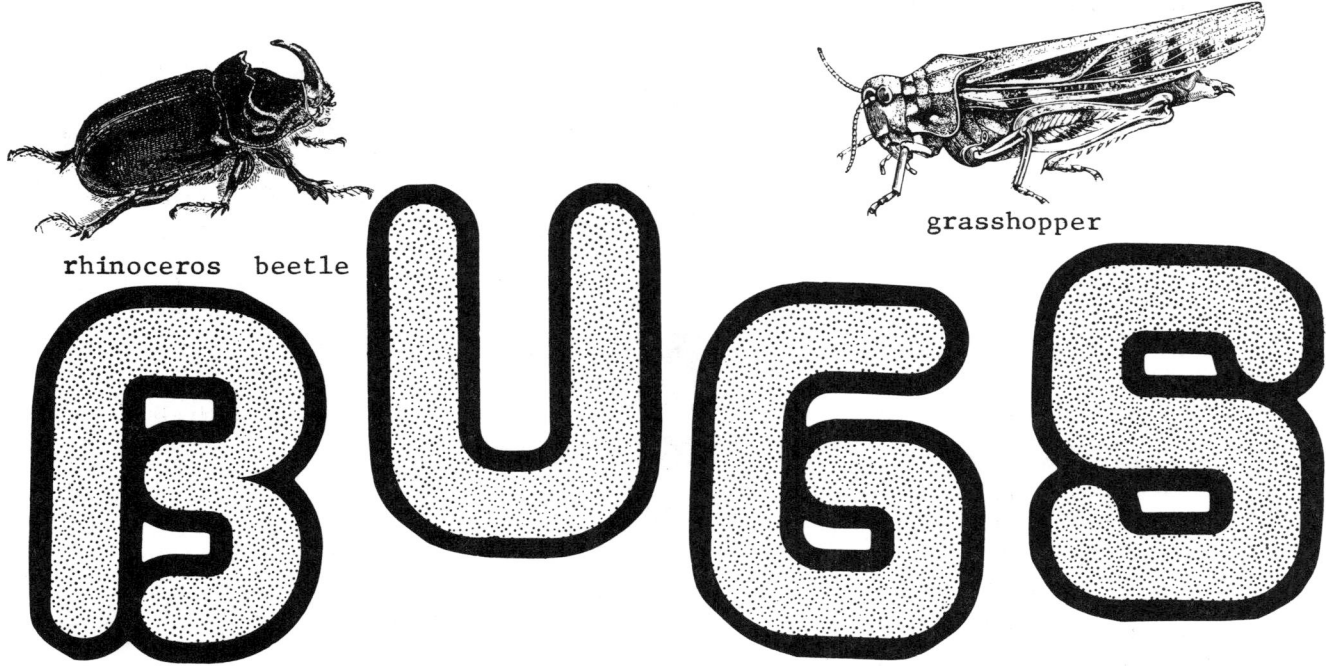

rhinoceros beetle

grasshopper

BUGS

Project Ideas: • report • photographs • slides •
• collections • reading lists • story •
• science fiction • museum exhibit • poster •

Seven-spotted Ladybirds (also known as Ladybugs)

Performing Arts

Classify...
Write a report on...
Interview someone who...
Compare one... to...
Hypothesize about...
Make a diorama of...
Take a field trip to...
Use a computer to...
Make a poster of...
Invent a...
Do a survey to find out...
Volunteer your services to...
Write a play...
Perform a play...
Write a song...
Sing a solo...
Form a musical group...
Collect oral history about...
Make a booklet of...
Draw a picture...
Collect...
Read poetry...
Write a poem...
Assemble a bibliography...
Write science fiction...
Write a fictional story...
Observe...
Experiment...
Write a letter to...
Redesign the...
Interpret...
Translate...

1. Read today's newspaper or watch a news broadcast on television. On a sheet of paper, list the _date_ and 5 items of news. One week from the date you listed, read the newspaper or watch a television news broadcast. Are any of the items still in the news?

2. Make a "Time Capsule". Put items of today's news into the capsule. Bury it.

3. Write a story in which someone finds a buried time capsule. The story can be an adventure or science fiction.

4. Write a newspaper — just the front page will be sufficient. Include a headline, several items of national and local news.

5. Visit a newspaper publishing company. Watch a newspaper being printed.

6. Invite a newspaper reporter to be a guest speaker for your class. After listening to the guest speaker, answer these questions:
   1. *What does a reporter do?*
   2. *What training does it take to be a reporter?*
   3. *Would you like to be a reporter? Why, or why not?*

NEWSPAPERS

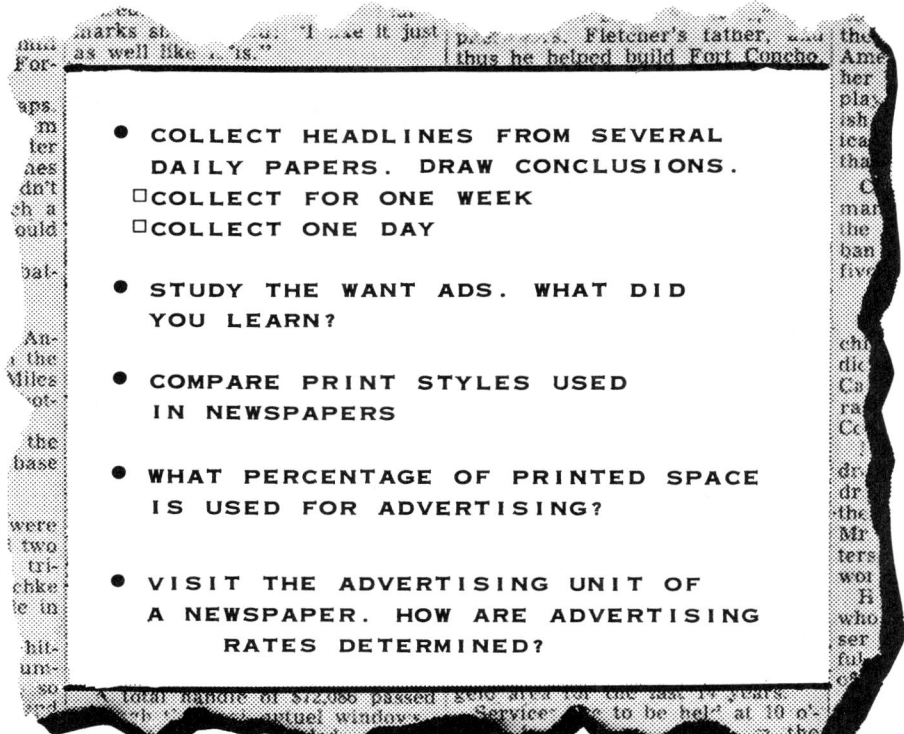

- COLLECT HEADLINES FROM SEVERAL DAILY PAPERS. DRAW CONCLUSIONS.
  - ☐ COLLECT FOR ONE WEEK
  - ☐ COLLECT ONE DAY

- STUDY THE WANT ADS. WHAT DID YOU LEARN?

- COMPARE PRINT STYLES USED IN NEWSPAPERS

- WHAT PERCENTAGE OF PRINTED SPACE IS USED FOR ADVERTISING?

- VISIT THE ADVERTISING UNIT OF A NEWSPAPER. HOW ARE ADVERTISING RATES DETERMINED?

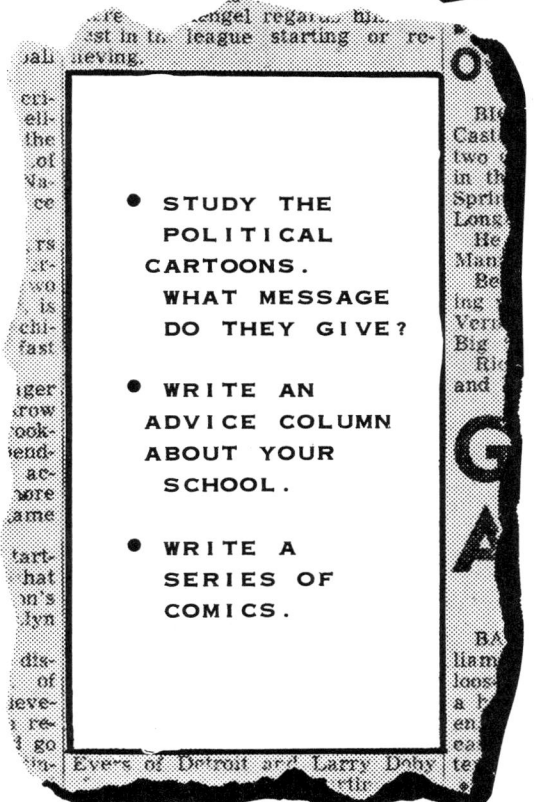

- STUDY THE POLITICAL CARTOONS. WHAT MESSAGE DO THEY GIVE?

- WRITE AN ADVICE COLUMN ABOUT YOUR SCHOOL.

- WRITE A SERIES OF COMICS.

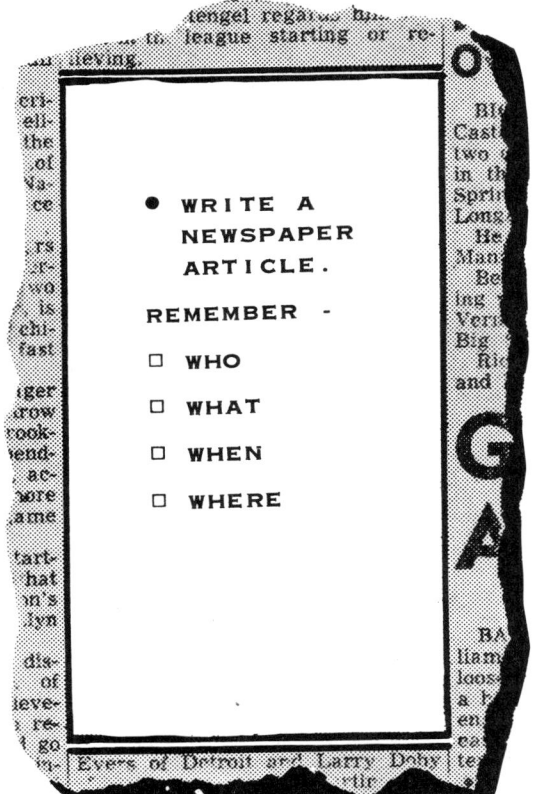

- WRITE A NEWSPAPER ARTICLE.

REMEMBER -

- ☐ WHO
- ☐ WHAT
- ☐ WHEN
- ☐ WHERE

> **Mnemonics** - *a memory technique: a word or set of letters which helps you remember something.*

Example:

> **Roy G. Biv** - *fictional name created to remember the colors and their sequence in a rainbow.*
>
> *R-red*
> *O-orange*
> *Y-yellow*
> *G-green*
> *B-blue*
> *I-indigo*
> *V-violet*

Another example:

> **Every Good Boy Does Fine** - *a sentence to remember the letter names of a musical staff.*

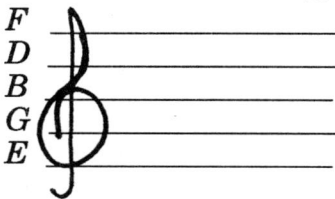

Create your own mnemonic(s).

Student Projects - Ideas & Plans. © Leadership Publishers,1994

Titles which Identify People

Here are some titles:

    Sir

    Lady

    Madame President

    Lord

    Your Honor

Add others titles:

Looking at Magazines

This activity can be repeated with many types of magazines and subject matter. Looking at magazines helps students to:
1. generalize about content matter,   *4. practice summarizing skills,*
2. be observant,   *5. practice listening skills,*
3. expand knowledge in many areas,   *6. improve speaking skills.*

Fourth Grade Students
Back Row: Brad Bond   Keli Keith   Staci Osmond
Front Row: Brad Van Weelden   Chris Sampson   Paul Renaud

Step One

Each of the fourth grade students shown in the photograph was given a copy of TOWN AND COUNTRY magazine. They were told to look at the magazine for ten minutes. (A timer was set to alert us to the time.) As students looked at the magazine, they were to determine: *For whom is the magazine written?*

To answer the question, students were to look at and think about:
1. article titles,
2. pictures as part of the articles,
3. advertising in the magazine.

When the timer signalled that ten minutes were completed, the students agreed that TOWN AND COUNTRY magazine caters to <u>people with money.</u>

Their conclusion was based on
1. expensive jewelry, clothes, and furs shown in the pictures and in the ads,
2. large expensive house furnishings shown in the pictures,
3. coverage of charity balls and social events,
4. ads for expensive private schools and pets, such as miniature horses and Sharpei dogs.

Step Two

Students were asked the question: "What did you learn about TOWN AND COUNTRY magazine and about the lives of the rich?

Responses

KELI KEITH: I learned about expensive jewels. Only rich people can afford them.

CHRIS SAMPSON: Certain magazines are written for certain people. TOWN AND COUNTRY is for the rich. I saw ads for gold and diamonds.

BRAD VAN WEELDEN: The rich usually have great big houses. They are fancy.

PAUL RENAUD: There's a lot of bribes and promises, like when the ads say (or seem to say) "This will make your grandchild happy and love you more." The ads try to lead you into buying things. The rich have to finance (manage) their money and keep it on budget.

BRAD BOND: Most items cost $1000 or more. The book shows pets like pure white Sharpei pups. They cost a lot of money.

STACI OSMOND: They have shoes but they are so high priced, such as snake skin shoes for $700.

Step Three

Discuss the "merits" and "demerits" of being rich.

Author's Comment: The discussion revealed much jealous, envy, and resentment of the rich. We discussed that, as a society, we tend to dislike or mistrust the wealty, powerful, good-looking and smart. Further discussion addressed: "Why is this dislike, mistrust and resentment present?" "Are these attitudes good for us?"

Step Four

At the end of the discussion, the teacher asked: "Would you want to be rich?"

KELI KEITH: Yes. I could get expensive things, jewels, diamonds, and emeralds, and dresses. I'd put half of the money in the bank and save it.

STACI OSMOND: Yes. You could have bodyguards and servants to go buy theater tickets and anything else you might want.

PAUL RENAUD: Yes. I want to do some things that take money, like to go Paris, take a trip around the world. I'd buy a private yacht and cruise the shoreline of Norway. Then I'd buy a fast boat for out in the middle of the lake - probably Lake Michigan.

CHRIS SAMPSON: No. All the girls would be after me just for my money. If I ever get rich, I want to get rich by my job - not inherit it from my ancestors. Poor is O.K. if you have enough to eat.

BRAD VAN WEELDEN: No. Money doesn't always make you happy. If you had a lot of money, you could spend too much. Then you'd be in debt and you wouldn't have anything.

BRAD BOND: Yes. I'm going to buy a ranch and have lots of animals - all the kinds of animals you'd find outside. I'll have a mansion. The mansion and the ranch will be right outside of Dallas.

Student Projects - Ideas & Plans. © Leadership Publishers, 1994

Famous
People

Wolfgang Amadeus Mozart.

1. Study about a famous person.

2. Write a play about a well-known person.

3. Write a play about someone in your family.

4. Make flashcards about a group of famous persons.

5. Construct a Trivia Game about famous people you have studied.

6. Make a map of your country, state or province. Add the names of famous persons to that map showing the birthplace of that person.

7. Sing a song (one already known or make one up) about a famous person.

8. If you become famous, in what area might you achieve fame?

9. If you could visit with any person, alive or dead, with whom would you like to visit.

10. Pretend you are a famous person. List things you'd do throughout your day if you were truly that famous person.

11. Study your family tree. Are there persons who are or were well-known?

12. Designate 10 categories, such as medicine, poetry... List 10 famous persons in each category.

Student Projects - Ideas & Plans. © Leadership Publishers, 1994

Jazz

Jazz

1. Play some jazz.

2. Listen to jazz.

3. Write an essay:
   "Jazz music makes me..."

4. Interview a jazz musician.

5. Research the history of jazz.

6. Do free-hand drawings and doodles while listening to jazz music.

7. Prepare a demonstration or lecture which describes how jazz music differs from other kinds of music.

jazz

SCHOOL
NEWS

Today's information.

& REPORTS

Information from books and other sources.

& TALES

Fictitious accounts and folktales.

Student Projects - Ideas & Plans. © Leadership Publishers, 1994

Adventurers & Pioneers

NEWS

Today's information.

& REPORTS

Information from books
and other sources.

& TALES

Fictitious accounts and folktales.

Read about . . .
Classify . . .
Write a report on . . .
Take a field trip to . . .
Use a computer to . . .
Make a poster of . . .
Compare one . . . to . . .
Hypothesize about . . .
Make a diorama of . . .
Write a letter to . . .

Interview someone who . . .

Make a booklet of . . .
Draw a picture . . .
Collect . . .
Read poetry . . .
Write a poem . . .
Assemble a bibliography . . .
Interpret . . .
Translate . . .
. . . other . . .

Poetry

Student Project: poetry

▸*Quest for Knowledge*◂

Schools have teachers and janitors and administrators.
Schools should be a place of learning;
A place to satisfy a great yearning for knowledge.
Schooling continues into college, where the effervescent
quest for knowledge is further nourished and continued
into tomorrow after tommorrow after tomorrow...

ARNOLD BURGGRAAF

Student: ARNOLD A. BURGGRAAF

Arnie likes to read and write poetry.
He has also completed short courses in
music and art appreciation.

Arnie is now a senior in high school.

After studying the poetic style of e e cummings, Arnie wrote these two poems.

●S C H O O L●

yuck
u run
2 classes
u do
not und
er
st
and
u take
tests that
you'll
ne
ver
pass
school will
frust
ra
te your
brain.

ARNOLD BURGGRAAF

This poem may be read in
two styles: the words in
parentheses or the words
outside the parentheses.

▸LIVING AND LEARNING◂

life (learning)
is like
(is) going
to (the)
school
it's like
(road) a
path it
can lead
u (away)
2 a better
(from ignorance)
life

ARNOLD BURGGRAAF

Student Projects - Ideas & Plans. © Leadership Publishers, 1994

Interpret . . .

a song

a feeling

a gesture

a dance

a period of history

a movie

a smile

a mathematical formula

a poem

a book

a riddle

a secret code

Trees

1. Classify trees.

2. List trees local to your area.

3. List products made from trees.

4. Discuss the role of trees in daily lives.

5. Read poems about trees.

   What thoughts are expressed in the poems?

   6. Write a poem about a tree.

   7. Write a song about trees.

   8. Make a collection of dried tree leaves.

   9. List medicines made from trees.

   10. List diseases of trees.

   11. Discuss the statement,

      "Trees and dogs are man's best friends."

12. What are the benefits and tragedies of forest fires?

computers

Computer usage falls into three main categories:

1. _Programming languages_ — such as BASIC, LOGO...

2. _Word processing_ — those programs designed specifically for writers, editors, and printers.

3. _Preprogrammed software_ — programs developed to help you achieve specific results. Examples: graphics, simulation, musical composition, inventory records, and others.

1. Experiment with all three categories listed above. From this experimentation, determine which avenue of computer usage you wish to pursue.

2. Using programming (any language) construct a program, game, or demonstration which illustrates how that computer language is used. Review your program, game or demonstration with other students. Show the project as well as the printout of commands used to create the program, game or demonstration.

3. Learn one computer graphics program. Design something using that computer software.

4. Use a word processing program of your choice. Write a story and print it into book form.

5. Visit department and computer stores. Make a comparative chart listing: a) brand, b) cost, c)peripherals available, d) software available for each system, and e) any other specific information available.

6. After you have learned how to use a particular computer software program, teach another person (someone who _wants_ to learn it) how to use that program.

7. Write an essay describing the "love/hate" affair you have with your computer (if you have a love/hate relationship!)

8. Speculate and project: "Computers will change society in these ways..."

9. After you have used a computer for some time and feel comfortable using a particular program, write a paragraph (or more) completing this sentence: "Because I can use computers, I feel more confident and..."

10. List all jobs related (in any way) to computers.

Use a computer to . . .

1. Design a car.
2. Design a fabric pattern.
3. Calculate the speed of a falling star.
4. Predict the occurrence of the solar and lunar eclipse.
5. Write a story.
6. Write a play.
7. Set up bookkeeping accounts.
8. Calculate percentages of sales.
9. Calculate interest payments.
10. Catalog your books.
11. Compute income or sales tax.
12. Write a newspaper.

Kristin Kunzmann, of Clay Central / Everly School, wrote this story when she was in 2nd grade. Her interests include: reading, math, and drawing. She also collects rocks and shells. She has been writing stories since she was in first grade. Someday she would like to become an artist or singer.

Can you complete Kristin's story "Birthday Bummer"?

Birthday Bummer

Chapter I

Lizzie and Elizabeth were twins. Identical twins. They dressed alike, they looked the same, they had brown hair and blue-green eyes. They were short and they looked exactly alike. They were in second grade.

Of course, they weren't alike in all ways. Lizzie liked to read and write, while Elizabeth liked to play softball, tennis, soccer. Lizzie played dolls a lot. Elizabeth went to gymnastics. Lizzie liked English, reading, and penmanship. Elizabeth liked recess, P.E., and math. So you see, they weren't alike in all ways.

Their parents bought them everything. But why did they say that they were still unhappy?

*Kristin **did** write the rest of this story. And if you were writing it, how would you complete the story?*

Student Projects - Ideas & Plans. © Leadership Publishers, 1994

Memories...   Games...   Ideas...   Toys...

Favorites...   Friends...

Children

Student Projects - Ideas & Plans. © Leadership Publishers,1994

Photography

1. Learn to use a camera.

2. Take pictures of your friends.
   Put the pictures into a scrapbook.

3. Take a picture of nature in action.
   Write one paragraph about the
   picture you have taken. Nature in
   action can be: snowstorm, falling leaves,
   rain, sunset, and other natural events.

4. Mark a 4' x 4' square. Take 2-4 pictures
   of that area. Is there anything
   special in that small area?

5. Visit a newspaper office. Ask a reporter
   what type of camera the reporter uses.
   Ask the reporter to tell you what
   makes a good picture for the newspaper.

6. Visit a newspaper office. Ask to speak
   to the person who runs the presses.
   Learn from that person how a picture
   becomes printed in the newspaper.

7. Visit a photography shop. Interview the
   photographer. Ask 3 or 4 questions you
   would like to know about photography.

8. Pick up your favorite magazine. Study the
   pictures in that magazine. What do you
   learn from studying those pictures?
   What do the pictures tell you about
   the magazine?

9. Assemble a scrapbook of photographs that
   cover a specific event or time periods.
   An event could be a fair, wedding or
   party. A period of time could be a trip,
   vacation, or one month.

Take a field trip to . . .

1. a museum.

2. a new industry in your area .

3. a bakery .

4. a place of natural beauty .

5. visit with early pioneers in your area.

6. learn about an occupation you are interested in.

7. learn how foods are canned and shipped.

8. collect sample rocks or leaves.

9. see how students in another school do independent projects.

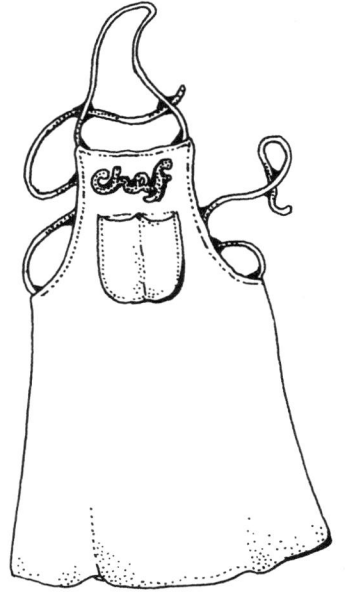

Juggling

1. *Watch a juggling act.*
2. *Learn to juggle.*
3. *Visit a juggler.*
4. *Perform a juggling act for friends.*

Balancing

1. *Watch a balancing act.*
2. *Learn to balance some object(s).*
3. *Perform a balancing act.*
4. *Interview someone who performs balancing acts. What did you learn?*

. . . . . *the i-d-e-a-l place to live* . . . . . .

Where is it located?

_____

Why is it ideal?

_____

_____

_____

_____

_____

_____

Would you have to move to live there? ❐ yes ❐ no

Use Computer Software to Complete a Project

Matthew Engelbert

Allen Mabee

Students:
Matthew Engelbert and Allen Mabee
use computer software to produce
editions of the <u>TUSCON SUN.</u>

One of the key features of the
<u>TUCSON SUN</u> is the sports report.

TUCSON ☀ SUN

JANUARY 28, 1987   EDITION LXXIX

WALRUSES FALL

(WALLA WALLA-AP) The Southwestern University of Tucson Zappies blew by the Walla Walla Walruses, 57-38, in a conference game Teusday night in Walla Walla.

The Walruses stayed close throughout the first half by trailing by three at halftime 21-18. A last second shot by Al Pine gave Tucson the momentum they needed into halftime. "I had the shot and i just had to take it and it swished," said Pine.

"Al was a big contributer tonight. I didn't think he'd play this well coming off his injury," Tucson Head Coach L.A. Kes said after the game.

In the second half Tucson broke the game wide open with a 20-4 spurt. They also out rebounded Walls Walla by 18-7. "We just played our hearts out that second half," Kes said, "we had to out rebound them and shoot better."

	FG-A	FT-A	RB	PF	TP
Al Pine	13-17	5-7	2	2	31
Joe Stump	4-8	4-8	11	4	12
Jim Jo Johnson	1-3	2-2	5	3	4
R.U. Young	0-0	0-0	0	0	0
Norm Perengen	2-3	2-4	7	4	6
Woody Lawrence	1-1	2-6	3	3	4

SUN ON FIRE

(TUCSON-AP) The offices of the Tucson Sun in the Sun building, went up in flames Friday afternoon. Police Chief Gus Tennyson claims the fire started in the main printing press.

There were no injuries in the blaze but many were taken to the nearest hospitals to be looked at.

The building was engulfed in flames by the time fireman arrived on the scene. "This is one of the worst fires in Tucson history," Fire Chief Charles Hotaman said. "We tried to save as much as we possible could. "The top seven floors of the 15 floor structure were destroyed. The seven floors contained the top floor of the Tucson Sun, an Arthur Murray dance studio, a fitness center, and television station KSON.

Owls

O W L S

1. Read about "Owls".

2. Classify owls.

3. Draw a picture of one or more owls.

4. Write a story in which the hoot of an owl *plays an important part.*

5. Listen to a tape or record of an owl's *hoot.*

6. Visit a zoo or wildlife refuge, or take a walk to see *live* owls.

7. Visit an ornithologist.

8. Study owl *feathers. Why can't you hear their wings flapping?*

9. What are owl *pellets?*

10. Make a poster about owls.

11. List all the helpful services the owl *performs.*

Each month has events and climatic conditions associated with it.

Events and climatic conditions vary from place to place.

Directions:
Make a set of posters which show events and/or climatic conditions associated with each month.
  Note: If you prefer, make four posters — one for each season — rather than a set of 12 posters — one for each month.

seasons

months

Sports

Read about. . .
Classify. . .
Write a report on. . .
Interview someone who. . .
Compare one. . . to. . .
Hypothesize about. . .
Make a diorama of. . .
Take a field trip to. . .
Use a computer to. . .
Make a poster of. . .
Invent a. . .
Do a survey to find out. . .
Volunteer your services to. . .
Write a play. . .
Perform a play. . .
Write a song. . .
Sing a solo. . .
Form a musical group. . .
Collect oral history about. . .
Make a booklet of. . .
Draw a picture. . .
Collect. . .
Read poetry. . .
Write a poem. . .
Assemble a bibliography. . .
Write science fiction. . .
Write a fictional story. . .
Observe. . .
Experiment. . .
Write a letter to. . .
Redesign the. . .
Interpret. . .
Translate. . .
. . .other. . .

Student Projects - Ideas & Plans. © Leadership Publishers,1994

Student Project

Students: **CAMERON BLINN** and **MARTIN GEURTS** designed the game HAUNTED HOUSE.

GAME TITLE: HAUNTED HOUSE

PURPOSE OF GAME: be the first to enter and exit the Haunted House.

TYPE OF GAME: board game.

NUMBER OF PLAYERS: any number

PROCEDURE: player rolls dice to move along the board. Obstacles are at certain places on the board.

OBSTACLES :

CLOSET OF HANDS - dark closet with hands grasping you.

PANTRY OF SPIDERWEBS - small room with spiderwebs that keep growing and expanding.

ROOM OF HORRORS - a room that has "things" that come at you.

BASEMENT OF GHOSTS- ghosts come and scare you.

and other adventures!

DESIGN A GAME

QUOTATIONS

1. Make a booklet of quotations.

2. Illustrate a quotation.

3. Prepare a one-person play based on the quotations of one person.

> "Art is man's refuge from adversity." Menander

4. Make a collage of quotations.

5. Form a discussion group which discusses quotations found in a particular newspaper or magazine.

6. Write your own "Book of Wisdom".

> A Japanese Proverb says, "Adversity is the source of strength."

7. Locate books of quotations in your library. Read some of one book.

8. Listen to speeches. How often are quotations interjected into the speech?

> "If you tell the truth, you don't have to remember anything." Mark Twain

> "A bore is a person who talks when you wish him to listen." Ambrose Bierce

> "A celebrity is a person who works hard all his life to become well known, then wears dark glasses to avoid being recognized." Fred Allen

puppets

1. List and describe kinds of puppets.
2. Watch a puppet show.
3. Make puppets.
4. Put on a puppet show.

Student Projects - Ideas & Plans. © Leadership Publishers, 1994

the HISTORY of MAN

1. Make a timeline to show major changes and progressions in man's history.

2. Write a play about man's early ways.

3. Write a "thank you" note (letter) to past ages for the improvements they made and passed on to us.

4. Read about early cave paintings. What did you learn?

5. Make a collage about man's history.

6. Make a game. The winner will be the first one to get from caveman to modern man.

The History of Man

Student Project <u>Sketching</u>

Student **JAMES HOWARD**, *fourth grade,*
sketches.

"The Owl" *J.Howard*

Project
WRITE TO THE AUTHOR

Lois Roets Ed.D.

Write to the author.

Describe your completed project.

Include your grade (or age) and address - if you wish a response.

Write to Dr. Lois Roets , c/o Leadership Publishers.

1. How do you define "THE WORLD"?

2. Name 3 global problems facing the world. Give _three_ solutions to _one_ of the problems.

3. Read about the "four corners" of the Earth — the world as we know it. After reading about them, list 25 facts or statements that are true about the entire planet EARTH.

4. Draw a political map of the WORLD or a portion of that world.

5. Make a products map of one country.

6. Prepare an exhibit showing how one section of the world differs from another section of the world, as far as climate and living conditions are concerned.

7. Read about the life of Mercatur, the mapmaker.

8. Read about and give a report on mapmaking.

9. Design a board game which would require participants to know on which continent each country is located.

10. Write a poem or song about a particular climatic area: tundra, tropics, wetlands...

11. Discuss: *"The world is shrinking."*

12. Write a science fictory story which describes how the world had to learn to cooperate so that all could survive.

FISHING

NEWS

Today's information.

&

REPORTS

Information from books

and other sources.

&

TALES

Fictitious accounts

and folktales.

Everyone wants
Justice

Directions:
Select a current issue. Identify the issue. Present two viewpoints of the issue.

Issue: _____

_____

Viewpoint One: _____   Viewpoint Two: _____

_____   _____

Conclusion _____

Stephanie Schwartz
Age 7, Corbett Elementary
Tucson, Arizona

Read the next seven
pages for procedures
for writing a book.
Follow them and you'll
have written a book!

Thanks, Stephanie, for
sharing this information!

HOW TO WRITE AND PUBLISH A BOOK by Stephaine Schwartz

Paper

I LOVE LIZARD By Stephanie Schwartz

ERASR

WORDS

yes

Dedication

I dedicate this book to

My Mom and Dad with love.

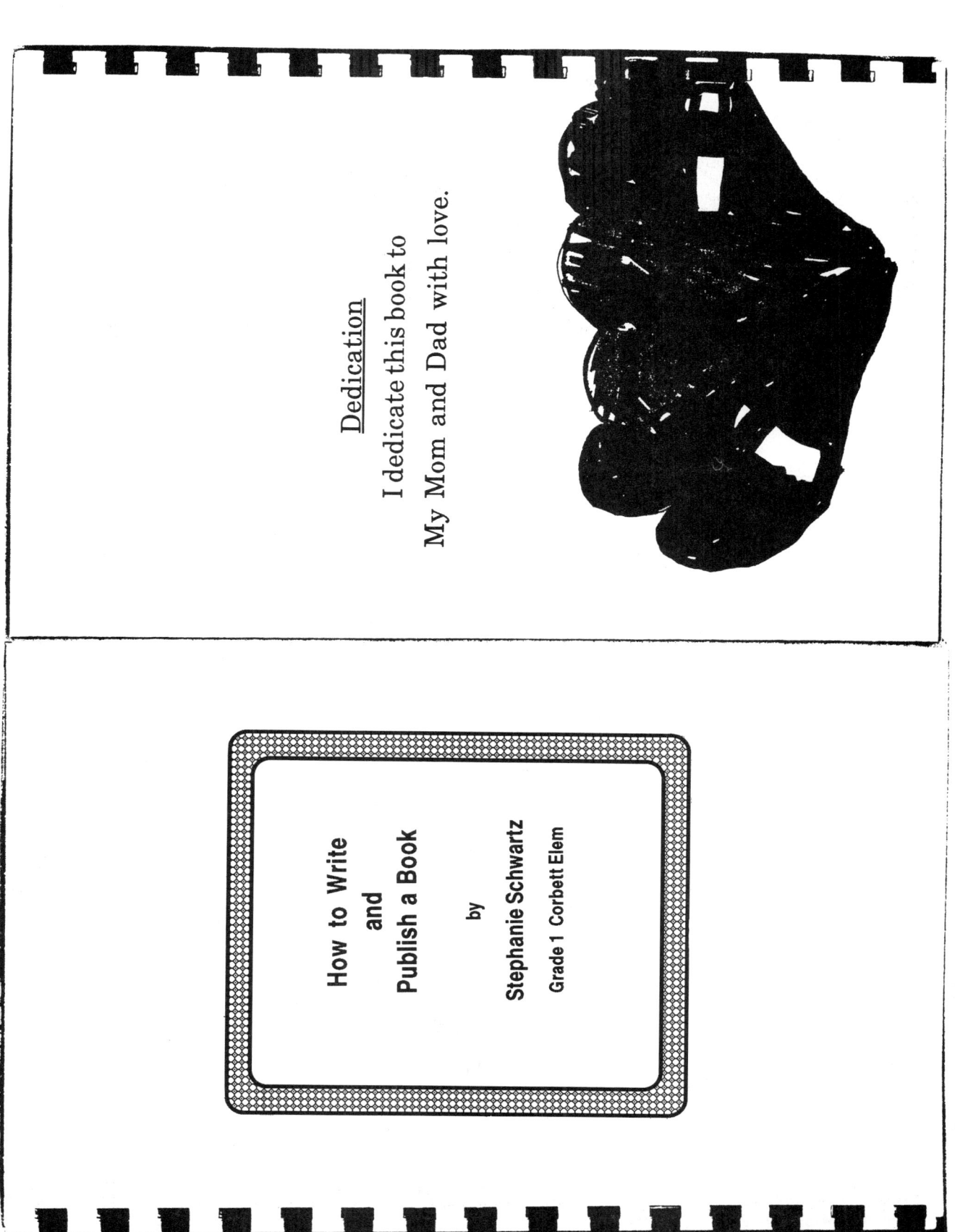

How to Write
and
Publish a Book

by

Stephanie Schwartz

Grade 1 Corbett Elem

Step 2. What characters do you want in your story? Maybe you want a princess in a castle or a poor person in a tiny house.

Step 3. What happens? For example, maybe a little girl got bitten by a rattlesnake and her parents couldn't afford to put her in the hospital.

Chapter 1 - How to Think of an Idea for a Story

Step 1. Choose scenery. The story might be on a prairie or a meadow, on the grasslands or on the beach. Maybe it is even by a stream.

If it is not a fantasy or fiction story, you would probably not like a scene.

Step 2. Get your ideas down on paper!!!

Chapter 2 - How to Start a Story

Step 1. Make a web of things you want to write about. A web helps you think of ideas that you want to keep in mind.

A web looks like this:

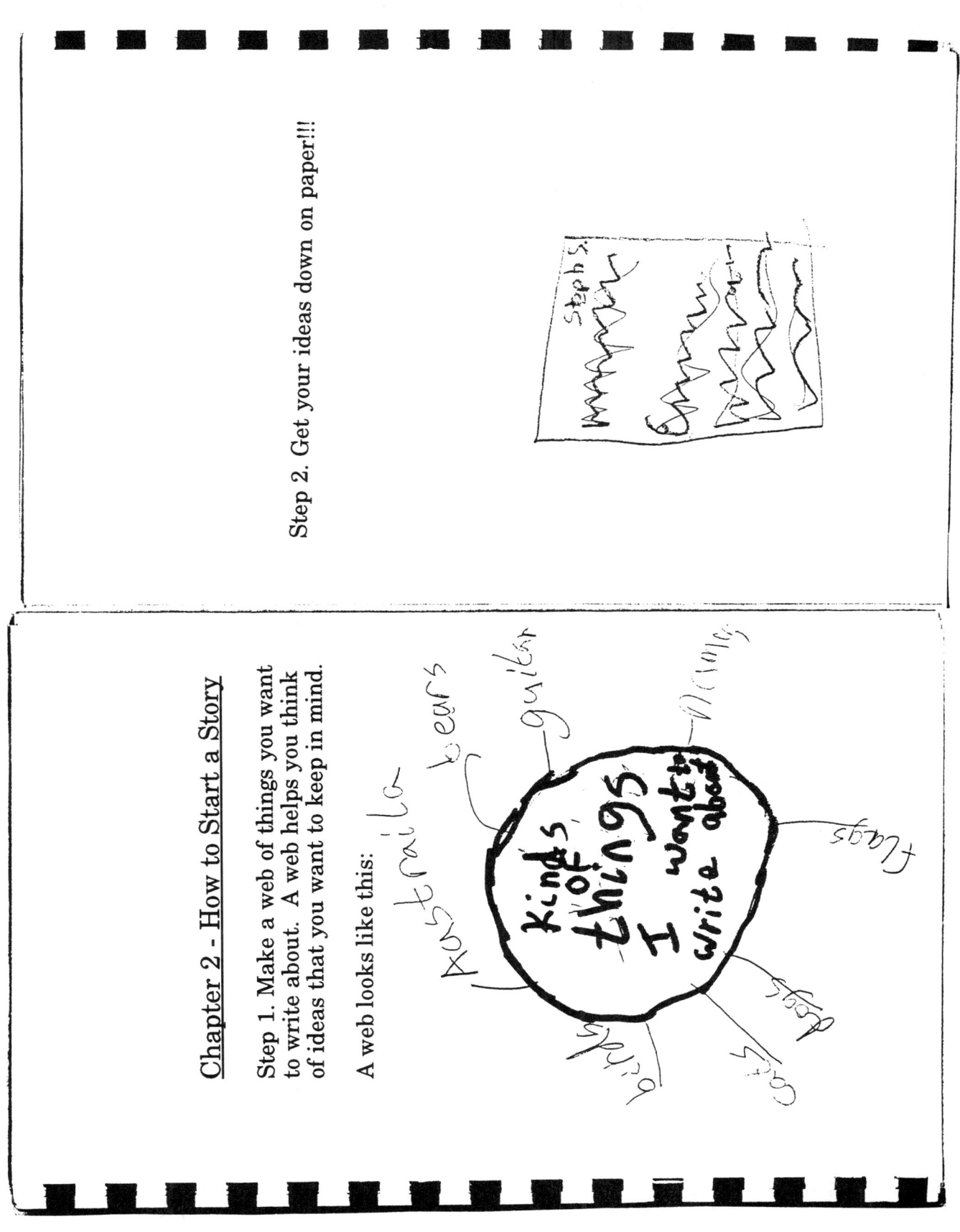

Chapter 4 - How to Finish Your Story

Step 1. Put an ending on your story. You might want to put into the back of your book an author's page.

Chapter 3 - How to Think of What Happens in Your Story

Step 1. Where is your story going to be placed at? For an example, it might be at a party, or at a basketball game. What comes to your mind after you write where it takes place? What comes to your mind is .... what happens!

Step 2. What environment is around your characters? That is another way to think of things to happen in your story. For an example, it means that the people in your story can be doing outdoor activities.

Student Projects - Ideas & Plans. © Leadership Publishers, 1994

Chapter 6 - Publishing Your Book

Step 1. Make a cover! To make a cover for your book you will need: cardboard or tagboard, markers, crayons, pen, pencil, colored pencil, and maybe some paints. Then pick out some of the materials. Then you might want to decorate with the materials that you picked out.

Step 2. Put your book together. To put your book together you will need binding and a binding machine.

Step 3. Send a copy of your story to a publisher and if that publisher thinks that your story has enough detail that you can understand, then he will publish it!

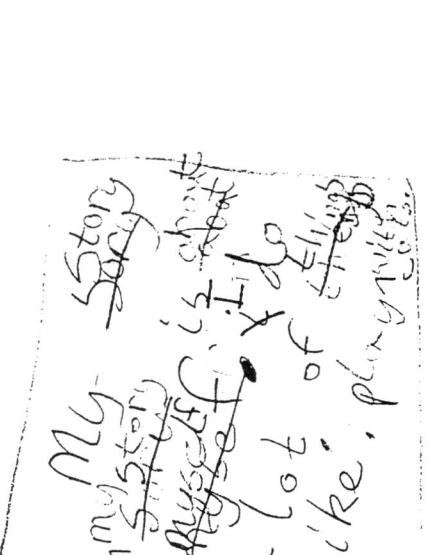

Chapter 5 - How to Edit and Revise Your Story

Step 1. Revise. Read what you have already written, and see if you left out any words in your story or information book. Then read your book to a friend or an adult to see if you need to add some details in your story. Then you should read your story to the same person and revise it again.

Step 2. Next you should get an adult to help you put the correct adult spelling and punctuation.

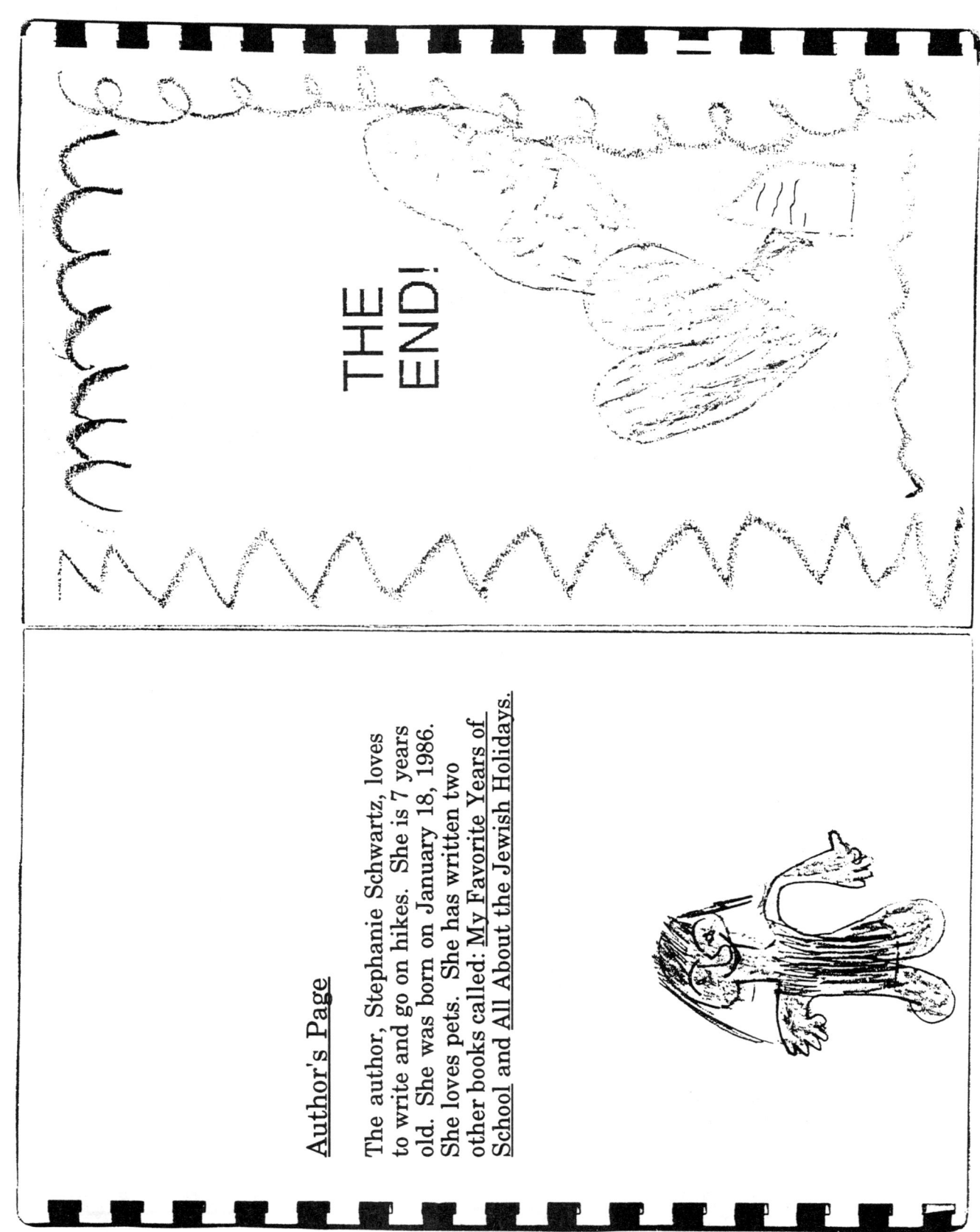

THE END!

Author's Page

The author, Stephanie Schwartz, loves to write and go on hikes. She is 7 years old. She was born on January 18, 1986. She loves pets. She has written two other books called: My Favorite Years of School and All About the Jewish Holidays.

WHY DO YOU
WANT TO GO?

HOW WILL YOU TRAVEL?

Take An

WHEN WILL YOU GO?

Imaginary Trip Around the World

WHAT WILL
YOU SEE?

WHAT WILL YOU TAKE
WITH YOU?

WHO WILL GO
WITH YOU?

WHAT ADVENTURES
WILL YOU HAVE?

HOW LONG WILL YOU
BE TRAVELING?

FLOWERS

Read about . . .
Classify . . .
Write a report on . . .
Interview someone who . . .
Compare one . . . to . . .
Hypothesize about . . .
Make a diorama of . . .
Take a field trip to . . .
Use a computer to . . .
Make a poster of . . .
Invent a . . .
Do a survey to find out . . .
Volunteer your services to . . .
Write a play . . .
Perform a play . . .
Write a song . . .
Sing a solo . . .
Form a musical group . . .
Collect oral history about . . .
Make a booklet of . . .
Draw a picture . . .
Collect . . .
Read poetry . . .
Write a poem . . .
Assemble a bibliography . . .
Write science fiction . . .
Write a fictional story . . .
Observe . . .
Experiment . . .
Write a letter to . . .
Redesign the . . .
Interpret . . .
Translate . . .
. . . other . . .

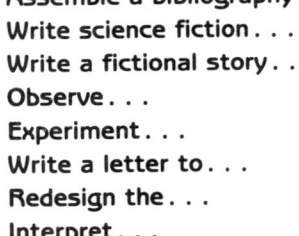

230

Do a survey to find out. . .

- public opinion
- cost differences
- viewpoints
- concerns
- kinds of products needed
- kinds of products offered
- kinds of services offered
- kinds of services needed
- amount needed
- amount used
- record changes over a period of time
- sample certain offerings.

Note to survey researchers:
When you conduct survey research, repeat the study (research project) to see if the same results occur. Repeating a research study or project is called <u>*replicating*</u> *a study.*

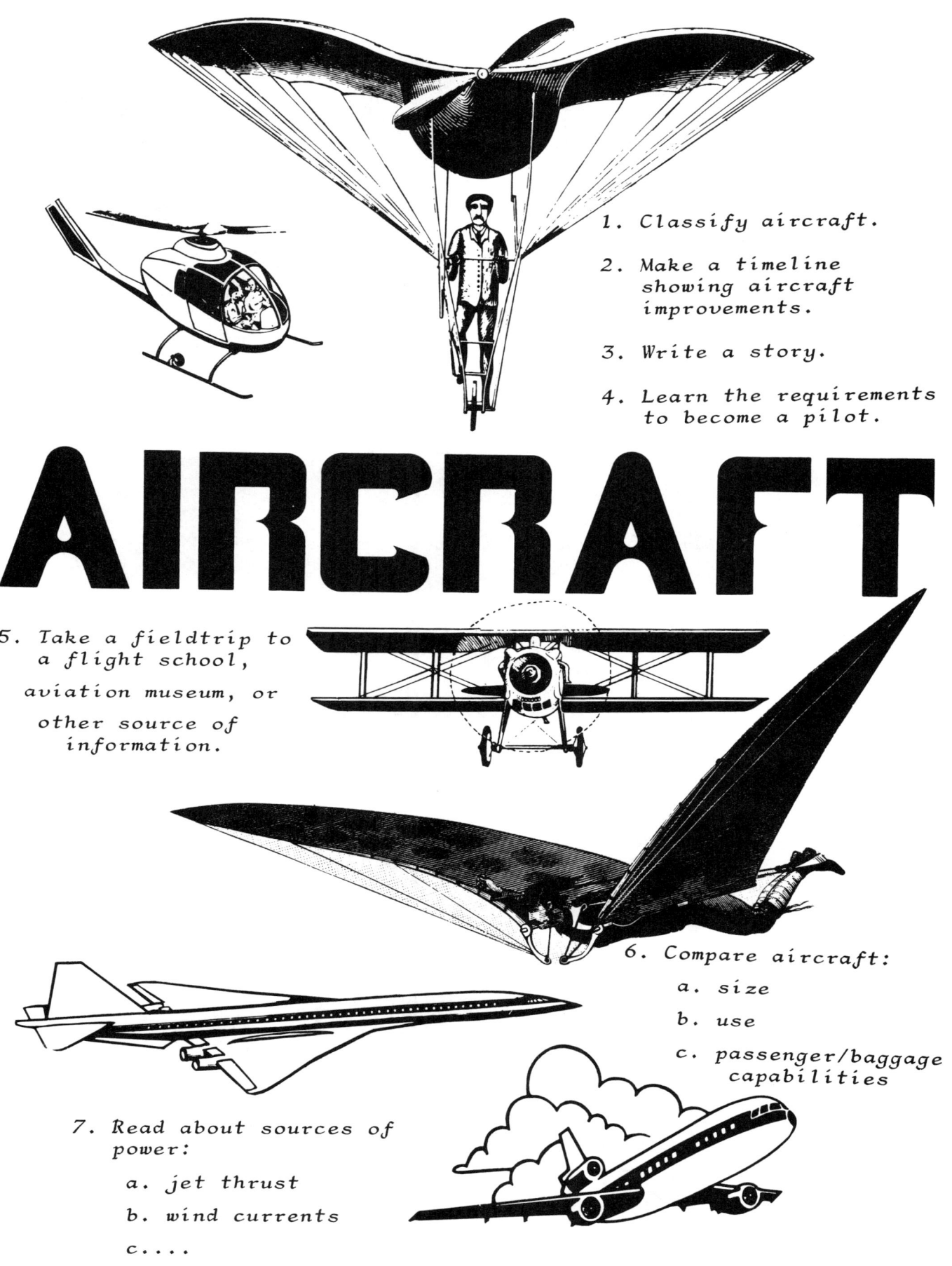

1. Classify aircraft.

2. Make a timeline showing aircraft improvements.

3. Write a story.

4. Learn the requirements to become a pilot.

AIRCRAFT

5. Take a fieldtrip to a flight school, aviation museum, or other source of information.

6. Compare aircraft:
   a. size
   b. use
   c. passenger/baggage capabilities

7. Read about sources of power:
   a. jet thrust
   b. wind currents
   c....

232

COMPARE

1. sunrise and sunset
2. popularity of television shows
3. warmth of mittens(gloves, hats...)
4. effectiveness of insect repellent
5. favorite "junk foods" of different
    age groups
6. softness of pillows
7. flavor of gum
8. comfort of shoes
9. the "sticking ability" of glue sticks
10. the calorie content of beverages
11. gas usage for different vehicles
12. cooking abilities of chefs
13. leisure time activities of teenagers
    in different geographic locations
14. the cost of postage since 1900
15. the water content in different snowfalls
16. the hardness of different woods
17. the taste of chocolates

Student Projects - Ideas & Plans. © Leadership Publishers,1994

Student Project

STUDENT: Jodi Hicks

PROJECT: Studying the Solar System

DESCRIPTION:
Jodi read about the Solar System with its planets, sun and moons.
Next, she made a poster.
She reviewed what she had learned with several groups of students.

Student Jodi Hicks
She is displaying one source of information.

OTHER PROJECTS RELATED TO <u>PLANETS</u> AND THE <u>SOLAR SYSTEM</u>:

1. Make a Trivia Game based on Solar System Facts.

2. Using papier-mache, make models of the planets.

3. Write a report on each planet.

4. Read about the discovery of each planet and moon.

5. Research: Which mathematical formulae are used to calculate solar and lunar eclipses?

6. Predict: What new discoveries will soon be made related to the universe.

7. Read a science fiction story based on colonizing other planets. Could all or part of the story <u>really</u> happen?

Student Projects - Ideas & Plans. © Leadership Publishers, 1994

BOATS ⚓ SHIPS

Read about . . .
Classify . . .
Write a report on . . .
Interview someone who . . .
Compare one . . . to . . .
Hypothesize about . . .
Make a diorama of . . .
Take a field trip to . . .
Use a computer to . . .
Make a poster of . . .
Invent a . . .
Do a survey to find out . . .
Volunteer your services to . . .
Write a play . . .
Perform a play . . .
Write a song . . .
Sing a solo . . .

Form a musical group . . .
Collect oral history about . . .
Make a booklet of . . .
Draw a picture . . .
Collect . . .
Read poetry . . .
Write a poem . . .
Assemble a bibliography . . .
Write science fiction . . .
Write a fictional story . . .
Observe . . .
Experiment . . .
Write a letter to .
Redesign the .
Interpret . . .
Translate . .
. . . other . .

WATER

1. What is it?
2. How is it formed?
3. Describe it:
   beauty...
   power...
   danger...
   advantage...
   disadvantage...
   softness...
   movements...

Redesign the . . .

typewriter

running shoes

high chair

rocking chair

roller skates

automobile

kite

parachute

tree house

tent

room you stay in

seating arrangement of your classroom

pencil and pen

bubble gum

bicycle

vacuum cleaner

broom

television

camera

school bus

Student: *Joe Strobel*

Project: *Making a Poster*

Description: *Joe selects a topic and then plans the poster.*

After the main theme is planned, Joe finds pictures and writes short descriptions and titles to complete the poster.

After the poster is completed, Joe covers the front with clear Contact Paper to protect the poster from moisture, dust or dirt.

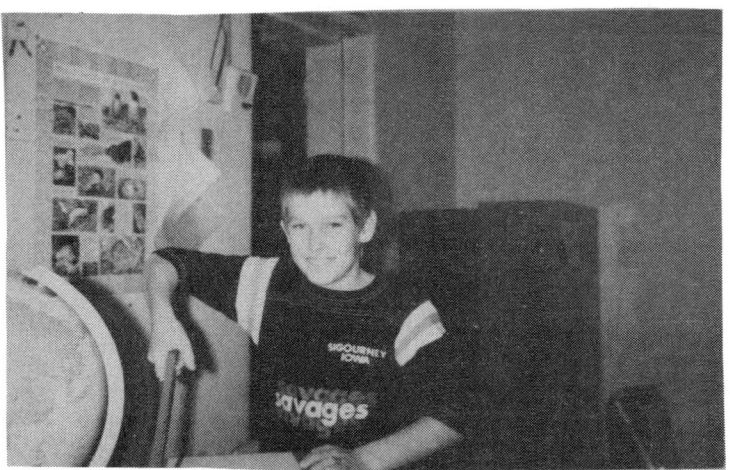

Poster-maker: *Joe Strobel*

Joe says: *"I like making posters. They look nice when they are finished.*

" I also like writing funny plays and acting them out."

Joe Strobel has been making posters and other independent or small group projects since he was in the second grade.

REPTILES

Read about...
Classify...
Write a report on...
Interview someone who...
Compare one... to...
Hypothesize about...
Make a diorama of...
Take a field trip to...
Use a computer to...
Make a poster of...
Invent a...
Do a survey to find out...
Volunteer your services to...
Write a play...
Perform a play...
Write a song...
Sing a solo...
Form a musical group...
Collect oral history about...
Make a booklet of...
Draw a picture...
Collect...
Read poetry...
Write a poem...
Assemble a bibliography...
Write science fiction...
Write a fictional story...
Observe...
Experiment...
Write a letter to...
Redesign the...
Interpret...
Translate...
...other...

"Reading makes the full man;
Conference a ready man; and
Writing an exact man."
OF THE ENTERTAINMENT OF BOOKS
by Jeremy Collier

- BOOKS BY YOUR FAVORITE AUTHOR
- NEWSPAPERS
- MAGAZINES
- COOK BOOKS
- MYSTERIES
- SCIENCE FICTION
- ADVENTURE
- ROMANCE BOOKS
- CURRENT EVENTS
- FORTUNE COOKIES
- ENCYCLOPEDIAS
- HISTORY BOOKS
- SCIENCE BOOKS
- CROSSWORD PUZZLES
- BILLBOARDS
- ROAD MAPS
- AD BROCHURES
- TRAINING MANUALS
- 'HOW TO' BOOKS
- COMIC BOOKS
- NONFICTION BOOKS
- NATURE BOOKS

240

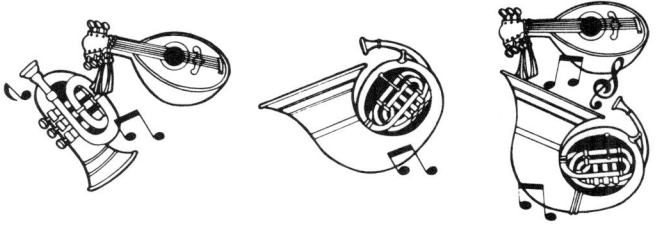

1. READ A BIOGRAPHY ABOUT A COMPOSER.

2. LISTEN TO WORKS OF ONE COMPOSER.

3. MAKE A MATCHING TEST - LIST COMPOSER ON ONE SIDE AND COMPOSITION ON THE OTHER.

4. LISTEN TO YOUR FAVORITE COMPOSITION OVER AND OVER. WHY DO YOU FIND IT SO SATISFYING?

5. ATTEND A CONCERT.

6. MAKE A POSTER HONORING YOUR FAVORITE COMPOSER.

7. LISTEN TO AUDIOCASSETTES WHICH DESCRIBE THE COMPOSER'S LIFE AND SOME COMPOSITIONS.

Composers

241

exercise &

Gymnastics

Read about . . .
Classify . . .
Write a report on . . .
Interview someone who . . .
Compare one . . . to . . .
Hypothesize about . . .
Make a diorama of . . .
Take a field trip to . . .
Use a computer to . . .
Make a poster of . . .
Invent a . . .
Do a survey to find out . . .
Volunteer your services to . . .
Write a play . . .
Perform a play . . .
Write a song . . .
Sing a solo . . .
Form a musical group . . .
Collect oral history about . . .
Make a booklet of . . .
Draw a picture . . .
Collect . . .
Read poetry . . .
Write a poem . . .
Assemble a bibliography . . .
Write science fiction . . .
Write a fictional story . . .
Observe . . .
Experiment . . .
Write a letter to . . .
Redesign the . . .
Interpret . . .
Translate . . .
. . . other . . .

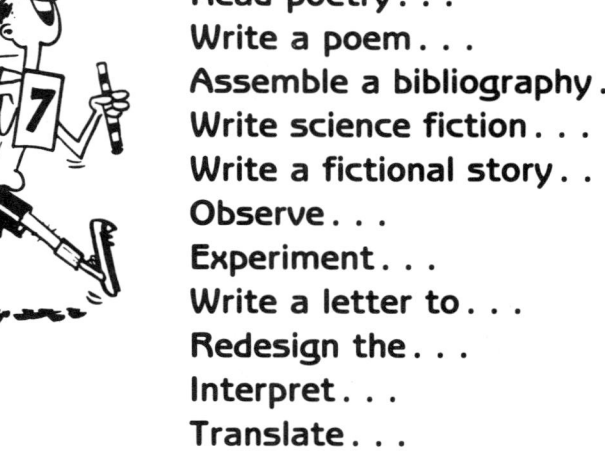

1. Make a dictionary of terms and symbols related to astrology.

2. What are <u>horoscopes</u>? Do you believe them?

3. Interview classmates. Do they believe in horoscopes?

4. What is the history of the <u>Zodiac?</u>

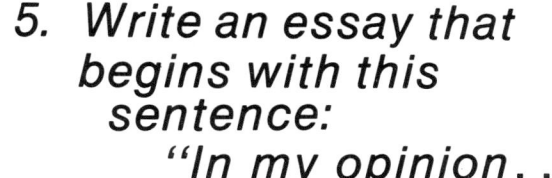

5. Write an essay that begins with this sentence: "In my opinion..."

Space Adventure (a play)

This play was written by Mike Winegardner (right) and Brad Colligan (left). Both were in the 2nd grade when they wrote and performed this play. The teacher helped the students write the play into the computer.

CHARACTERS:
Astronaut Winegardner
Alien Colligan
Narrator
Control Tower

SETTING: An astronaut is going to travel in a space shuttle. His destination is the moon.

TIME: 1975.

PROPERTIES:
blastoff button
space shuttle
space suit
alien suit
metors of various size (crumpled paper loosely taped together)
wad of "bubble gum" (large wad of pink sponge or similar substance)
blanket

***** the play *****

NARRATOR: As we join our astronaut, he is in the shuttle and ready to switch the "blast off" button. (Astronaut pushes button) He pushes the button and the ten second countdown begins.

CONTROL TOWER: 10. 9. 8. 7. 6. 5. 4. 3. 2. 1. We have lift off! (Sound effects of liftoff)

NARRATOR: Our astronaut is bound for the moon. He adjusts the controls, and gets ready for a long ride to the moon.

ASTRONAUT: (adjusts controls) We're bound for the moon. I'll just set these controls (does so) and all will be fine. (astronaut falls asleep)

NARRATOR: Our astronaut does not know it, but something is about to happen. As he sleeps, a meteor shower is headed towards him. (one meteor hits the shuttle. Astronaut quickly awakens and reaches for radio control)

ASTRONAUT: Astronaut Winegardner to control tower. Winegardner to control tower. Come in. Come in, control tower. Come in!

CONTROL TOWER: Come in Astronaut Winegardner.

ASTRONAUT: Trouble. A meteor shower. I've been hit once. Can't tell how much damage is done. I think....

NARRATOR: But the meteor has hit an important part of the ship. Part of the right engine that controls the communications systems, has been damaged. Our astronaut is cut off from any contact with the control tower. He is on his own in a vast universe.

ASTRONAUT: (clicking the control buttons) Control Tower? Control Tower? I can't hear you. (Another meteor hits) Oh, no! My communication system is gone.

NARRATOR: Our astronaut doesn't know it but he has been knocked off course. He was going to the moon, but now he is headed for the planet Mars.

ASTRONAUT: My ship is going towards a red fiery ball. I can see it coming. I didn't know the moon looked red. *(stares into space)* That isn't the moon. That is Mars, the red planet. I'm heading towards Mars and have no way of stopping the ship.

CONTROL TOWER: Control Tower to Astronaut Winegardner. Where are you? Radio your position immediately. Please, radio your position. We cannot help you if we don't know where you are.

NARRATOR: But no message from Control Tower reaches the Astronaut. No communications can be sent or received.

ASTRONAUT: I must land. I hope I land in one piece and that my space ship doesn't crash *(pause and gives a "jerk" as if the ship has landed)* I am here - on Mars. *(looks around)* So long as my air supply tank is full, and my food supply lasts, I will be able to live.

ALIEN: *(sees space ship, walks around it, knocks on ship)* Hm-m-m, what have we here? It looks like a piece of junk, an overgrown pumpkin, or a humongous Frisbee. Or, it could be a space ship. *(looks at the ship again)* It's not a space ship. It is a Frisbee. *(tries to pick it up)* Oh, this is a very heavy frisbee.

ASTRONAUT: *(sees alien)* What is this "thing" I see outside my window? I thought there was no life on Mars. But this thing is trying to pick me up. Well, I will have to speak to "it" or "him" or "her" - or whatever it is.

ASTRONAUT: *(calls to Alien)* Hey, you! What are you trying to do?

ALIEN: Pick up this big Frisbee. I love playing with Frisbees. This is the biggest Frisbee I have ever seen. It will be fun to throw it.

ASTRONAUT: This is not a Frisbee! This is a space ship. I am Astronaut Winegardner and this is my ship. What or who are you?

ALIEN: This isn't a Frisbee? Oh, that's too bad.

ASTRONAUT: I repeat, who are you? I am a human, Astronaut Winegardner. I come from planet Earth. Are you an alien?

NARRATOR: But no message from Control Tower reaches the Astronaut. No communications can be sent or received.

ASTRONAUT: I must land. I hope I land in one piece and that my space ship doesn't crash *(pause and gives a "jerk" as if the ship has landed)* I am here - on Mars. *(looks around)* So long as my air supply tank is full, and my food supply lasts, I will be able to live.

ALIEN: *(sees space ship, walks around it, knocks on ship)* Hm-m-m, what have we here? It looks like a piece of junk, an overgrown pumpkin, or a humongous Frisbee. Or, it could be a space ship. *(looks at the ship again)* It's not a space ship. It is a Frisbee. *(tries to pick it up)* Oh, this is a very heavy frisbee.

ASTRONAUT: *(sees alien)* What is this "thing" I see outside my window? I thought there was no life on Mars. But this thing is trying to pick me up. Well, I will have to speak to "it" or "him" or "her" - or whatever it is.

ASTRONAUT: *(calls to Alien)* Hey, you! What are you trying to do?

ALIEN: Pick up this big Frisbee. I love playing with Frisbees. This is the biggest Frisbee I have ever seen. It will be fun to throw it.

ASTRONAUT: This is not a Frisbee! This is a space ship. I am Astronaut Winegardner and this is my ship. What or who are you?

ALIEN: This isn't a Frisbee? Oh, that's too bad.

Student Projects - Ideas & Plans. © Leadership Publishers, 1994

ASTRONAUT: I repeat, who are you? I am a human, Astronaut Winegardner. I come from planet Earth. Are you an alien?

ALIEN: I am the human. You are the alien. I live here. You are the one that just dropped in - so to speak.

ASTRONAUT: O.K. No point arguing about it. (aside to audience) Until I know how strong this guy is, I had better not argue with him. (turns to speak to Alien) O.K. We are both human and we are both aliens. Now that we got that straight, now can you help me get back to Earth?

ALIEN: Did you bring any Frisbees?

ASTRONAUT: That's not the point. The point is, how do I get back to Earth?

ALIEN: Are you sure you don't have any Frisbees? And, how come you want to go so soon? You just got here.

ASTRONAUT: (sighs wearily) It's been a long day. I like you but I want to get back to Earth. My space ship needs repairs. Anybody here know anything about repairing a space ship?

ALIEN: I am the champion Frisbee thrower. I am also the ...

ASTRONAUT: (interrupts Alien) I don't need a Frisbee thrower! I need someone who can repair my space ship.

ALIEN: You interrupted me. I was going to tell you that, not only am I the champion Frisbee thrower, I am also the champion space ship repairman.

NARRATOR: Together they repaired the space ship.

ALIEN: (to audience) I have a plan for going to Earth. I'll put this big wad of super-duper bubble gum on the big Frisbee - which this guy calls his space craft. I'll hang on to the super-duper bubble gum. And I'm on my way!

ASTRONAUT: (calls to Alien) I think I am ready to go. Good-bye. Thanks for your help.

ALIEN: Good-bye. You can be on your way. (Alien pretend to walk away but puts the bubble gum onto the ship. Alien grabs hold of the gum to begin the ride to Earth)

NARRATOR: The astronaut takes off. He does not know that the Alien is attached to his space ship. The super-duper bubble gum is holding the Alien to the space ship.

ASTRONAUT: (calls to control tower) Astronaut Winegardner to Control Tower. Astronaut Winegardner to Mission Control Tower. Come in, Mission Control Tower.

CONTROL TOWER: This is Mission Control Tower. I hear you. I hear you loud and clear. Come in, Astronaut Winegardner. Give your location.

ASTRONAUT: I am nearing the orbit of Earth. I shall be landing in just a few minutes. I just passed Halley's comet so I should be coming in soon.

CONTROL TOWER: Good. Your landing pad is ready and clear. Over and out.

NARRATOR: It looks like all is clear. But as the space craft lands, the Alien's bubble gum falls off. The Alien bumps to the ground and the space ship slides on the gooey gum. The Astronaut and the Alien find themselves sitting, face to face, outside the space ship.

ASTRONAUT: (sees Alien) What are you doing here? I thought you were back on Mars.

ALIEN: (looks sad) Don't be mad at me. I just wanted a ride on your Frisbee. And I wanted to see what kind of Frisbees you had on Earth. Don't be mad at me.

Student Projects - Ideas & Plans. © Leadership Publishers, 1994

Space Adventure page 4

ASTRONAUT: Oh, all right. You're here so we might as well make the best of it. Come on, I'll take you ... *(Alien interrupts)*

ALIEN: Help! I'm getting hot. Quick. Hold up a blanket for protection. I'm getting so hot. I'm going to self-destruct. A blanket. Quick! *(Alien and Control Tower hold up blanket which prevents audience from seeing the Alien)*

NARRATOR: As soon as the blanket prevents anyone from seeing the Alien, there was a loud explosion. *(sound of explosion)*

ASTRONAUT: That's the end of the Alien. Poor little guy. All he wanted was to see what kind of Frisbees we had on Earth.

ALIEN: *(peaks around the corner of the blanket - he has shed the costume of the alien)* Hello, folks. I am an alien no longer. I am really an Earth person.

ASTRONAUT: You look like an Earth person. How did you get to be an alien on Mars?

ALIEN: An evil warlord captured me, changed what I looked like, and sent me to his prison. His prison was Mars, the red planet.

ASTRONAUT: How long did you have to stay in prison on Mars?

ALIEN: I had to stay until some honest and kind person set me free. You are that kind generous person.

NARRATOR: And both have been happy ever since.

ALL TOGETHER: The end.

INFORMATION BOX

*A hypothesis is an idea, explanation, or theory which explains or interprets
a set of facts or circumstances.*

A hypothesis is an idea, not a proven fact.

Hypothesize about . . .

1. the origins of the earth.

2. the future of the universe.

3. the outcome of the next World Series.

4. the election of the next president or prime minister.

5. cure for cancer, AIDS or another disease.

6. the possibility of another Ice Age.

7. next "tragedy" to happen on your favorite television soap opera program.

8. the effect of rising costs for housing on low-income families.

9. the long term results of anti-smoking campaigns.

10. the results obtained if a president, prime minister, attorney general or judge thinks he/she can break the law while performing official duties.

11. the exercise of aggressive acts of one government upon another government.

12. the possibility for world peace if everyone spoke the same language.

Read poetry...

√ *associated with a particular period of history.*

√ *associated with a particular occupation.*

√ *that describes sunrise and sunset.*

√ *that makes you feel happy.*

√ *written by local poets.*

√ *that tells of nature.*

√ *written by your favorite poets.*

Following the reading, you may wish to illustrate the poem, or interpret the poem through dance, mime or song.

bibliography. . .

INFORMATION

BIBLIOGRAPHY

1. *list of books written by one author*

2. *list of books published by one publisher*

3. *list of books about one topic*

4. *list of books and other readings about a topic*

Assemble a bibliography. . .

titles published by a particular publishing company

magazines you regularly read

particular group of people

mystery stories

nature books

favorite author

trivia books

science facts

Transportation

Identify modes of transportation.

Trace the history of transportation.

Compare modes of transportation:
comfort, cost, speed, safety, ...

List all types of transportation you have used.

Create a timeline for transportation.

What will future transportation look like?

Your topic of choice:

Transportation

BALLET

1. Read the history of ballet.

2. Each ballet movement or pose is completed with the feet in one of five positions. Learn the five positions.

3. Make a dictionary of ballet terms.

4. Read the "story-line" about the major ballets. THE NUTCRACKER SUITE tells the story of a nutcracker who comes to life. What are other stories for ballets?

5. Invite a ballet dancer to visit you. Listen to what is said; watch the steps and movements the ballet dancer makes.

6. Research: Which composers have written music for the ballet?

7. How does ballet differ from other forms of dance, such as tap, ballroom and other traditional dance forms?

8. Read about some famous ballet dancers. although there are many, you may wish to read about Rudolph Nureyev, Mikhail Baryshnikov, Anna Pavlova, and George Balanchine.

Read about . . .
Classify . . .
Write a report on . . .
Interview someone who . . .
Compare one . . . to . . .
Hypothesize about . . .
Make a diorama of . . .
Take a field trip to . . .
Use a computer to . . .
Make a poster of . . .
Invent a . . .
Do a survey to find out . . .
Volunteer your services to . . .
Write a play . . .
Perform a play . . .
Write a song . . .
Sing a solo . . .
Form a musical group . . .
Collect oral history about . . .
Make a booklet of . . .
Draw a picture . . .
Collect . . .
Read poetry . . .
Write a poem . . .
Assemble a bibliography . . .
Write science fiction . . .
Write a fictional story . . .
Observe . . .
Experiment . . .
Write a letter to . . .
Redesign the . . .
Interpret . . .
Translate . . .
. . . other . . .

RELIGIONS

1. Read the "Religion" entry in an encyclopedia.
   After reading the "religion" section, do <u>one:</u>

   a. Discuss, with an interested person, your
      thoughts as you read the "Religion" section.
   b. Read the "Religion" entry in another
      encyclopedia. Are the entries similar?
   c. List 10 (or more) facts you learned while
      reading.

2. Arrange a panel of three or more persons who will
   discuss the value of religion:
   a) to them personally and/or 2) to society-at large.

3. Compare several religions. Use these points
   (and others — if you wish) for comparison:
   a. doctine or chief beliefs
   b. code of conduct for daily living
   c. required rituals or ceremonies
   d. stories or recorded history.

4. List many religions. Be
   certain to include religions
   from all areas of Earth.

5. Identify sacred objects, places, or feastdays, and
   the religion associated with them.
   Examples: Ganges River — Hindu religion
   Christians — the BIBLE
   SEDER — ceremonial feast of the
   Jewish people

6. List <u>religion</u> and the <u>person</u> acknowledged
   as the founder of that religion.

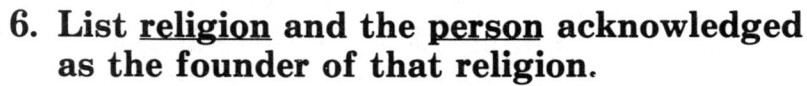

7. Do a survey of your town or
   city. How many religions
   are represented?

WOODCUTS ARE AN EXPRESSIVE FORM OF VISUAL EXPRESSION.

LEARN HOW WOODCUTS ARE MADE.   MAKE A WOODCUT. MAKE COPIES OF IT.

WOODCUTS

This book is used by teachers, students and parents.
Therefore, the teacher guide is included as well as sample student responses.
Oh, yes, and pictures of students in action!

Congratulations, Mr. Peyton, students and the community of Gillette, Wyoming!

"Triple-dissection" Unit developed by teacher, Bill Peyton,
Conestoga & Meadowlark Elementary Schools   Gillette, WY

Program Description

The following unit is a "natural" for busy classroom teachers wanting more hands-on activities without extensive preparation and clean-up. It is very popular with parents and administrators as well because children are highly enthused. The unit is productive, low-key and from the School of Life.

Mr. Peyton's academically-gifted students love their triple-dissection unit because it's fun and easy, explores things most people have never seen, and allowed them to think in ways seldom before experienced. It's natural for youngsters to take things apart. Why not make this productive and use the child's curiosity?

The unit has three parts of about 10 days each: Appliances, Boingers, Bodyworks. Teachers may reduce the number of days and still benefit, as knowledge-of-content at the elementary level may not be as important as attitudes, feelings, insights that become major concepts and the joy of learning for learning's sake.

In classes of 6-10 students, we dissected:
✔ Appliances,
✳ Boingers (stringed musical instruments),
❖ Bodyworks.

✔ Appliances.
Parents, townspeople, merchants.... donate small used appliances in various states of disrepair. Typewriters, mechanical adding machines, poorly-made fans and record players are especially plentiful in our changing culture.

The teacher first provides simple tool training, then students slowly work their way deep into the appliance of choice. Library research is best done during this phase, as it's more meaningful. Sometimes items get repaired or altered in function, and that's okay. Putting the item back together is also beneficial, if only to retrace steps. No harm done.

Most appliances have significant evolutionary development. They're created during a long series of trial and errors. And where is the unit's concept headed? Is the student going in this direction, too? If a typewriter becomes electrified and is connected to a computer which is also advancing, what is next? Will the grown-up student someday be interfacing his mind with computer circuitry - without benefit of wires? It's possible!

✳ Boingers (musical instruments). Music is another "natural" for us all, yet we barely tap into its educational powers. Old pianos and other stringed instruments are easy to obtain through word-of-mouth and free radio advertising. Many school districts will provide free transportation for heavy items to be used in the classroom. Students methodically take apart the instruments and in so doing begin to understand them. Research becomes more relevant in the process. Finally, the youngster produces a sound-making instrument. Various spin-off projects may result such as placing a tray of water on vibrating strings or rolling up a "megaphone" for amplification. ▶▶▶

❖ <u>Bodyworks</u>. After dissecting appliances and musical instruments, what could be more natural than examining a formerly-living creature? It's the ultimate appliance!

Youngsters learn about their own bodies through the examination of lesser creatures. ("Lesser" becomes questionable as the wonders of a worm's lips or the beautifully-webbed feet of a frog are put on display under microscopic conditions.)

Elementary teachers may obtain free small animals from "leftovers" from junior/senior high school dissection classes, or order them from a biological supply house. Some teachers don't pass up 'roadkill', as there is much to learn from the way a badger's hind feet are designed, or how beautiful a porcupine's quills may be. The teacher should obviously use sanitary methods for handling such animals. Rubber gloves are recommended. Students' curiosity about the tendons in an animal's leg, for instance, overcomes any reluctance to touch a dead leg.

Complex scientific dissection isn't necessary - just take apart a leg slowly like a cook does preparing chicken dinner. Let a piece of skin dry for a week and see how tough it is. Or, find the brain of a fish to see why they can't think.....

Students learn respect for their own bodies, overcome fears, do something "different", come to understand the miracles of nature - all by slowly dissecting critters. It works.

Comments by Mr. Peyton

In all three mini-units, the child becomes his own best teacher. The teacher serves as implementor, facilitator, coach, "idea-leader". Students do their own thinking best.

There is a special ironic twist in these units, personally. They were invented for academic high-ability students who needed high-challenge activities, but they are also highly suited to average learners who may be talented in areas other-than-academic.

Youngsters who lost interest in "book-learning" years before, suddenly become passionately involved in disassembling and re-assembling a projector. A girl finds delight in peeling off a frog's skin and making a drawing. Students may respond in many ways because of a wide variety of interests and talents.

We need to move our students into productive portions of our technical structure and support functions - sooner than the usual junior and senior high school. This "triple-dissection" unit served that purpose and many more. ●

The following pages show pictures of students in action.
The students also developed the unit "end-of-unit test". Some sample test responses are included. Note: these tests were originally hand-written. They are typed here so they fit onto one page. The sketches are photocopies of the originals.

Welcome ! Guess what? You get a quiz!   1. First question: what is your name?

I am: *Cassidy*

2. List any five appliances you worked on or SAW being worked on.

a) *VCR*   b) *Large Calculator*   c) *Film projector*   d) *Train*   e) *Typewriter*

3. BELOW, draw the one most interesting   4. Draw an <u>animal</u> being dissected.
to you. <u>Show plenty of parts exposed.</u>   <u>Show plenty of parts exposed</u>

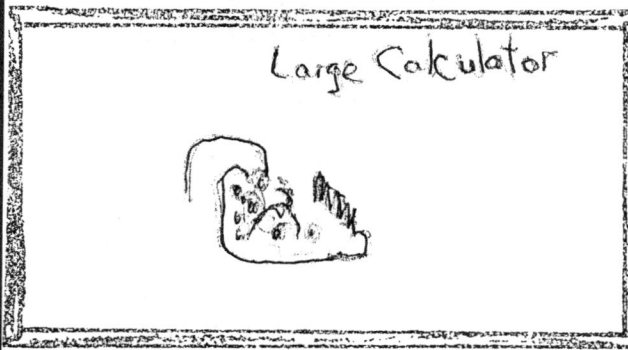

Name of appliance: *Large Calculator*   Type of animal: *Fish*

5. List any three <u>important</u> thoughts you have about your hospital visit.
That is, three important things you learned and have been thinking about.

a. *CAT SCAN. Complex computer with lots of knobs*

b. *Lab, blood and plasma, freezer*

c. *Physical therapy, exercise bike with leg weight pusher*

6. Look around this room. Name two <u>objects</u> (things) that are interesting to you.

a. *yellow paper - looks like Far Side*

b. *tamp*

7. Now choose one of these and tell why you find it interesting:

yellow paper. I like the Far Side

8. Name three professions (jobs) you may like to do when you grow up.
Give some thought before answering.

a. *Politician*

b. *Lawyer*

c. *Doctor*

Gillette, WY

A fifth-grader, Blake Johnson, in Gillette, Wyoming, manipulates a screaming drill while wearing safety glasses. He drills at an angle so the screw will be slanted. The wire must be very tight to make a good "boinging" sound. Students later attached huge coffee cans or a guitar amplifier to the boinger boards, producing strange and wonderful sounds.

PRIDE OF CRAFTSMANSHIP is shown by Joshua Williams and Shaun Helsper. They created their three-string boinger with a drill and did all the work themselves. The wires could be "tuned" by inserting a small board underneath the wires. The boys found out that placing the vibrating board on a tabletop produced a pleasing resonance. Well, a resonance anyway!

DISSECTING AN OLD CALCULATOR is child's play for David Anderson and Joshua Williams. The power screwdriver saves time as long as the operator remembers "lefty loosy, righty tighty". Calculators and typewriters are especially easy to find and have many fascinating intricate parts. Plus -- what could be more natural to children than taking something apart? Sometimes the trick is to (partially) put it back together. Then take it apart again!

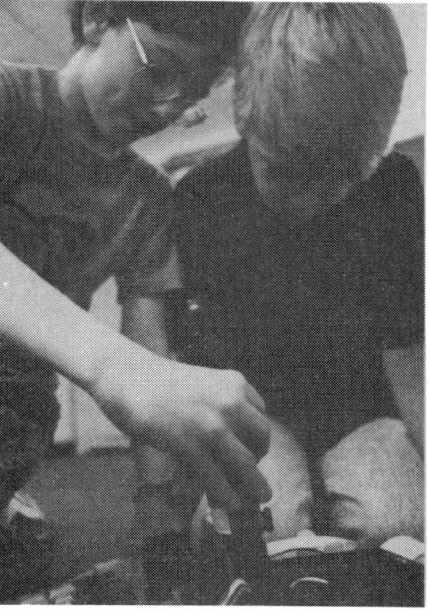

Welcome ! Guess what? You get a quiz!   1. First question: what is your name?

   I am: *Mandy*

2. List any five appliances you worked on or SAW being worked on.

   a) *Piano*   b) *VCR*   c) *TV*   d) *Typewriter*   e) *Calculator*

3. BELOW, draw the one most interesting   4. Draw an <u>animal</u> being dissected.
   to you. <u>Show plenty of parts exposed.</u>   <u>Show plenty of parts exposed</u>

Name of appliance: *Piano*   Type of animal: *Fish*

5. List any three <u>important</u> thoughts you have about your hospital visit.
   That is, three important things you learned and have been thinking about.

   a. *What was behind the cafeteria.*

   b. *What it was like in surgery.*

   c. *Inside the CAT SCANning computer*

6. Look around this room. Name two <u>objects</u> (things) that are interesting to you.

   a. *Dissection kit*

   b. *Animals we're dissecting*

7. Now choose one of these and tell why you find it interesting:

   Animals because you can see the body parts.

8. Name three professions (jobs) you may like to do when you grow up.
   Give some thought before answering.

   a. *Animal training*

   b. *Veterinarian*

   c. *Doctor (children's doctor).*

(Gillette, WY)

Student Projects - Ideas & Plans. © Leadership Publishers, 1994

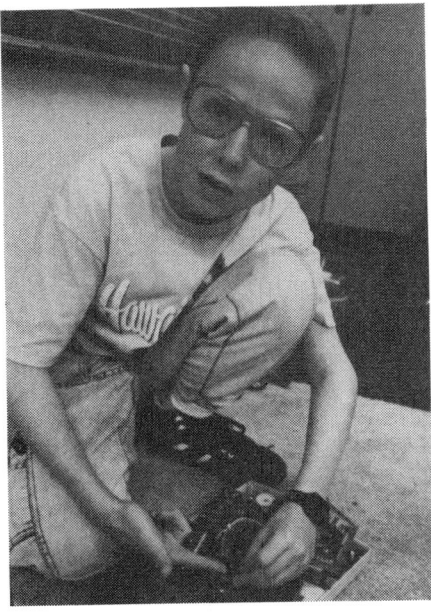

HEY! THIS TELEPHONE has the same basic circuitry as a radio! Jake Sinclair's face shows the wonder of discovery in dissecting an appliance unit, all of which will be "history" when he's grown. Yet the seeds of knowledge are hereby planted. After taking this trashed telephone home for homework, he brought it back in small pieces, spread them across the rug and -- the telephone still worked (sort of). Many appliances have a long evolutionary history. We know what it was and what it is now. But what will it become?

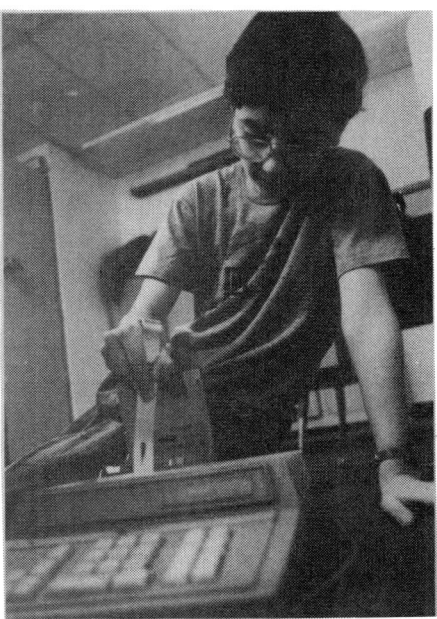

Meadowlark Elementary fifth-grader, David Anderson, gently inserts a pry bar in an unplugged calculator donated by a parental bookkeeper. He took apart other calculators and noticed many differences in older models, yet many similarities -- the evolution of an idea. What will the calculator of the future be like? Perhaps an implant under our skins wired to the brain? Who knows? David says <u>he</u> knows, but he's not telling .... yet.

Welcome ! Guess what? You get a quiz!   1. First question: what is your name?

                                                    I am: *J.R. Nies*

2. List any five appliances you worked on or SAW being worked on.

     a) *TV*   b) *VCR*   c) *Typewriter*   d) *Radio*   e) *Calculator*

3. BELOW, draw the one most interesting   4. Draw an <u>animal</u> being dissected.
   to you. <u>Show plenty of parts exposed.</u>   <u>Show plenty of parts exposed</u>

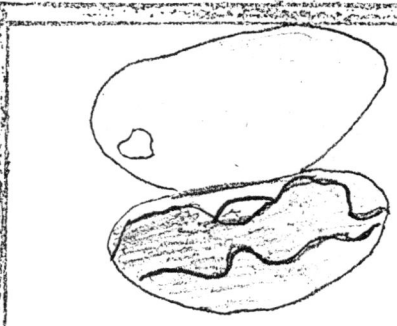

Name of appliance: *Television*   Type of animal: *Mussle*

5. List any three <u>important</u> thoughts you have about your hospital visit.
   That is, three important things you learned and have been thinking about.

     a. *CAT SCAN takes x-rays that are like cross sections and you can see tissue.*

     b. *X-ray machines pick up certain metals really good.*

     c. *If a person got a bad burn they would go to the emergency room.*

6. Look around this room. Name two <u>objects</u> (things) that are interesting to you.

     a. *the old typewriter*

     b. *the bones on top of the cupboard*

7. Now choose one of these and tell why you find it interesting:

        The typewriter is interesting because it is way different than modern ones.

8. Name three professions (jobs) you may like to do when you grow up.
   Give some thought before answering.

     a. *Doctor*

     b. *Computer programmer*

     c. *Lawyer*

(Gillette, WY)

THE GANG'S ALL HEAR making and listening to boinger boards manufactured from old piano wires. This lively group of sixth graders at Conestoga Elementary School in Gillette, Wyoming, learned tool use in the process of having fun. Four boards can be seen, each with sounds as individual as its creators. Smaller boingers can be made from stringed instruments smaller than an old piano, of course, or one may simply purchase guitar wire and string it up. Many things can be done with the vibrating wires, such as plucking them while immersed in water or taping a pencil on the wire and "writing" its frequency.

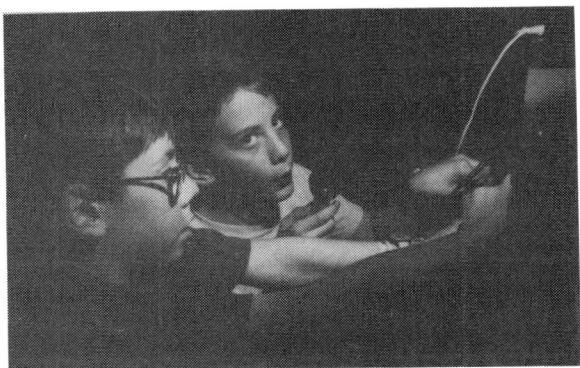

WHISTLING IN THE DARK, sixth-graders Benjamin Taylor and Cassidy Bertalot create an audio-visual delight. They took a junked oscillator (donated by the school district) and hooked it up to an amplifier. Then a beat-up microphone was plugged in to the amp. Wow! Even when whistling the same pitch, the Gillette students discovered how different their mouths were. The oscillator showed very different patterns. Later, they put the microphone under boinger wires and plucked strings, to investigate varied frequencies on the oscillator. You don't have to have fancy equipment to do projects. Students will find many possibilities to explore with junked appliances. It's a good idea to cut the power cord first.

(Gillette, WY)

Welcome ! Guess what? You get a quiz!   1. First question: what is your name?

I am: *Tanya*

2. List any five appliances you worked on or SAW being worked on.

a) *VCR*   b) *Slide projector*   c) *Video tape*   d) *Film projector*   e) *Calculator*

3. BELOW, draw the one most interesting to you. <u>Show plenty of parts exposed.</u>

4. Draw an <u>animal</u> being dissected. <u>Show plenty of parts exposed</u>

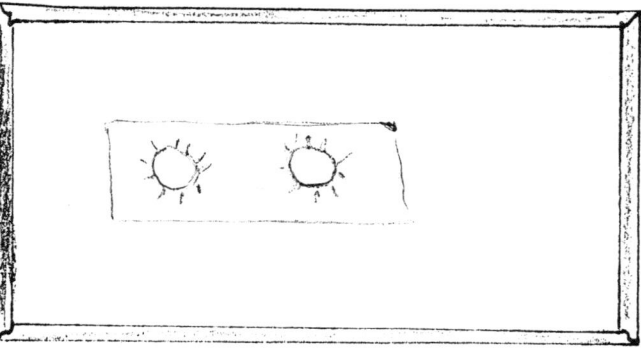

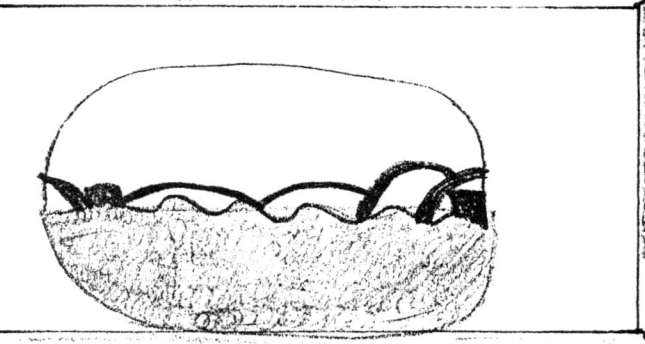

Name of appliance: *Video tape*

Type of animal: *Clam mussel*

5. List any three <u>important</u> thoughts you have about your hospital visit. That is, three important things you learned and have been thinking about.

a. *How they deliver babies.*

b. *How they take blood tests.*

c. *What they do for a broken bone.*

6. Look around this room. Name two <u>objects</u> (things) that are interesting to you.

a. *Old typewriter*

b. *Tape recorder*

7. Now choose one of these and tell why you find it interesting:

The old typewriter. I like it because it is old and it would be neat to take it apart.

8. Name three professions (jobs) you may like to do when you grow up. Give some thought before answering.

a. *Lawyer*

b. *Doctor*

c. *Pediatrician*
    d. *Teacher*

(Gillette, WY)

264

Welcome ! Guess what? You get a quiz!

1. First question: what is your name?

   I am: *Holly*

2. List any five appliances you worked on or SAW being worked on.
   a) *Typewriter*   b) *Piano*   c) *Radio*   d) *Tape recorder*   e)*VCR film thing*

3. BELOW, draw the one most interesting to you. <u>Show plenty of parts exposed.</u>

4. Draw an <u>animal</u> being dissected. <u>Show plenty of parts exposed</u>

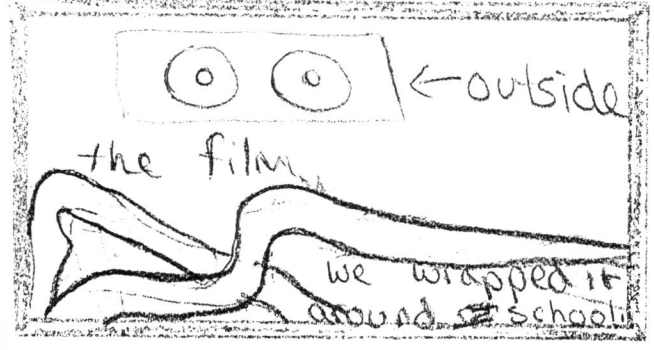

Name of appliance: *VCR film*

Type of animal:

5. List any three <u>important</u> thoughts you have about your hospital visit. That is, three important things you learned and have been thinking about.

   a. *Physical therapy - the helpers or physical therapists try to always be cheerful. They don't want their patients grouchy.*

   b. *CAT SCAN - they can tell if anything is wrong with anyone - even a baby. The inside of the C.A.T. Scan is really awesome.*

   c. *Bloom Room. The blood goes through a long process before it is stored in the blood refrigerator.*

6. Look around this room. Name two <u>objects</u> (things) that are interesting to you.
   a. *Calendar on the bulletin board*
   b. *The pyramid of coffee cans (under the table)*

7. Now choose one of these and tell why you find it interesting:
   The calendar has beautiful pictures and is very creative.

8. Name three professions (jobs) you may like to do when you grow up. Give some thought before answering.

   a. *I want to be a nurse to help people in pain or cheer them if they are sick.*

   b. *I also may be an elementary teacher. I love to hear the cries of joy after a child learns to read.*

   c. *Or, I want to be an author and illustrator, because I love and enjoy writing stories and drawing pictures.*

(Gillette, WY)

Welcome ! Guess what? You get a quiz!   1. First question: what is your name?

I am: _____

2. List any five appliances you worked on or SAW being worked on.

a) _____   b) _____   c) _____

d) _____   e) _____

3. BELOW, draw the one most interesting to you. <u>Show plenty of parts exposed.</u>

4. Draw an <u>animal</u> being dissected. <u>Show plenty of parts exposed</u>

Name of appliance: _____   Type of animal: _____

5. List any three <u>important</u> thoughts you have about your hospital visit. That is, three important things you learned and have been thinking about.

a. _____

b. _____

c. _____

6. Look around this room. Name two <u>objects</u> (things) that are interesting to you.

a. _____

b. _____

7. Now choose one of these and tell why you find it interesting:

_____

8. Name three professions (jobs) you may like to do when you grow up. Give some thought before answering.

a. _____   b. _____   c. _____

Gillette, WY

Identify.....   *Locate on maps*.....   *Research occupation related to* ....
Sing about ....   *Research people living on*.....   *Describe*......   *Draw* .....

M   **M**
O   **O**
U   **U**
N   **N**
T   **T**
A   **A**
I   **I**
N   **N**

R   **R**
A   **A**
N   **N**
G   **G**
E   **E**
S   **S**

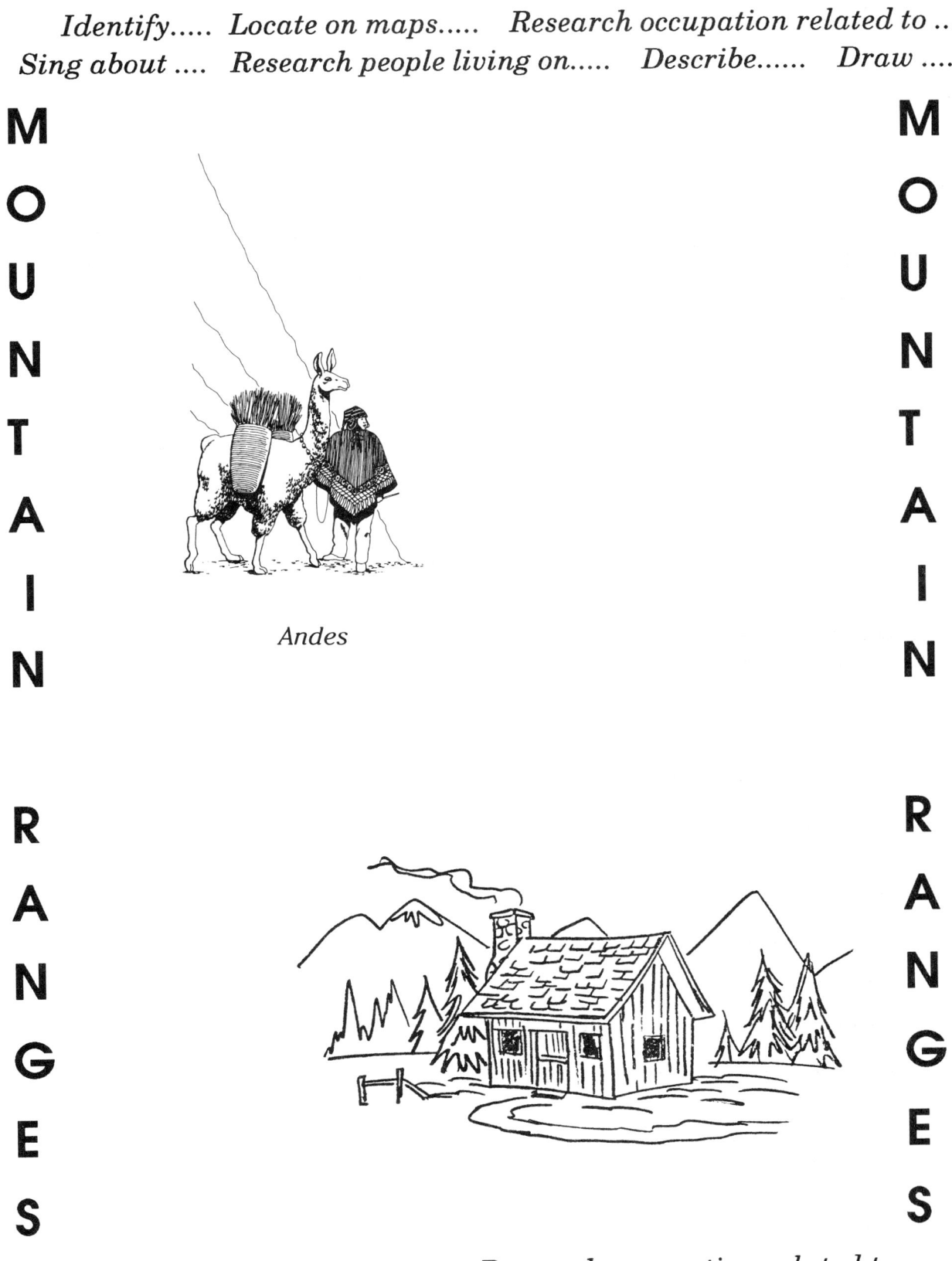

Andes

Identify.....   *Locate on maps*.....   *Research occupation related to* ....
Sing about ....   *Research people living on*.....   *Describe*......   *Draw* .....

Mythology

Read about . . .
Classify . . .
Write a report on . . .
Interview someone who . . .
Compare one . . . to . . .
Hypothesize about . . .
Make a diorama of . . .
Take a field trip to . . .
Use a computer to . . .
Make a poster of . . .
Invent a . . .
Do a survey to find out . . .
Volunteer your services to . . .
Write a play . . .
Perform a play . . .
Write a song . . .
Sing a solo . . .
Form a musical group . . .
Collect oral history about . . .
Make a booklet of . . .
Draw a picture . . .
Collect . . .
Read poetry . . .
Write a poem . . .
Assemble a bibliography . . .
Write science fiction . . .
Write a fictional story . . .
Observe . . .
Experiment . . .
Write a letter to . . .
Redesign the . . .
Interpret . . .
Translate . . .

Archeology

Read about . . .

Classify . . .

Write a report on . . .

Interview someone who . . .

Compare one . . . to . . .

Hypothesize about . . .

Make a diorama of . . .

Take a field trip to . . .

Use a computer to . . .

Make a poster of . . .

Invent a . . .

Do a survey to find out . . .

Volunteer your services to . . .

Write a play . . .

Perform a play . . .

Write a song . . .

Sing a solo . . .

Form a musical group . . .

Collect oral history about . . .

Make a booklet of . . .

Draw a picture . . .

Collect . . .

Read poetry . . .

Write a poem . . .

Assemble a bibliography . . .

Write science fiction . . .

Write a fictional story . . .

Observe . . .

Experiment . . .

Write a letter to . . .

Redesign the . . .

Interpret . . .

Translate . . .

. . . other . . .

Waterfalls

1. Identify well-known waterfalls.
   Example: Angel Falls- 2648 feet - Venezuela

2. Write a story about water going over the falls.

3. Research:

   How are waterfalls created?
   List several explanations.

   Do waterfalls remain the same size or length?

   Which waterfalls are tourist attractions?

   Which is the waterfall nearest you?

   What is the relationship between a waterfall
   and the land around it?

   Your research topic: _____

   _____

4. Have you seen a waterfall?
   If yes, describe it.
   If no, which waterfall would you like to see?

5. You are an engineer. Create a waterfall.

6. Paint a picture of a waterfall. *This can be*
   a realistic picture or abstract representation.

7. Try to imitate the sound of a waterfall.

Niagara Falls

270

1. Read a book about gardening.

2. Write a "how to" book of gardening.

3. Raise a flower garden.

4. Raise a vegetable garden.

5. Raise 3 kinds of the same vegetable.
   Which one — grows the best?
                 — tastes the best?
                 — is the easiest to grow?

6. Visit other gardens. What do you observe?

7. Weed control — "how much" and "with what".

8. Through cross pollination, develop a new variety of plant.

9. Raise a vegetable not ordinarily raised in your part of the country. Report on your efforts.

10. Certain states and companies promote certain "new" fruits or vegetables. Actually, the fruits or vegetables aren't new, they just are not very popular. Through advertising, more people use them. Examples: broccoli and kiwi fruit. Others?

EXPRESSIONS

How many facial expressions can you make? How many can you draw?

Student Projects - Ideas & Plans. © Leadership Publishers, 1994

Butterflies

1. Collect butterflies. Learn how to do it by asking someone <u>or</u> reading about the procedure in a book. Each specimen should be labeled.

2. In the summer or fall, take a walk through the woods or grasslands. How many butterflies did you count?

Moths

3. Describe the life cycle of a moth (or butterfly).

4. How can you tell the difference between a butterfly and moth?

5. Make a poster or chart on butterflies, moths, or both.

6. Read and report about the habits of a particular moth or butterfly.

7. Make a poster or chart showing the butterflies (or moths) from smallest to largest. Keep drawing scaled.

8. Visit a museum to see butterflies and/or moths. What thoughts went through your mind as you saw the specimens?

9. Using bits of fabric, paste and other odds and ends, make models of each phase of the lifecycle. Put signs by each model to identify and explain that part of the life cycle.

JUNGLE TROOPERS

A long time ago, in the Vietnam War, American soldiers captured a Chinese soldier. They forced him to tell them everything he knew. One of the things he told them was that there was a diamond hidden in the African jungle.

Five men wanted to go the jungle.

When they got to their boat, one man got in. It blew up. Then there were four.

These four headed for their airplane. One man got in. It blew up. Now there were three men.

These three finally got an airplane and headed for African. A big wind blew them off course and they were headed for Japan.

King Kong grabbed one man. Now there were two.

Two men got up. Three fighters for America joined them. Now there were five.

Godzilla grabbed two of them. And the three remaining walked and walked.

They finally reached the jungle. One fell off a bridge. And when he fell, he got shot too. The troops went on and on.

Author: ANDY GOODNER
Currently: 4th grade.
Story written when Andy was in second grade.

They finally found the cave. All of a sudden, a cheetah ran through and grabbed one, and went on until she was home with her kittens.

The one remaining man went in the cave, got the diamond and went back through the cave. This time, he had to go through a lot of snakes. He made it.

When he got in the middle of the jungle, br-r-r-r, a B-52 bomber blew up the jungle. The person died.

As for the cheetahs, they are safe. The diamond is still lost, and is

    gone
        forever.

Planning Forms

and

Sample Completed Planning Forms

My Project

Date _____

Student Name _____

Title or Description: _____

_____

Plan of Action:

_____

_____

_____

_____

_____

Use time from class: _____

✏️ *Evaluation --* ✏️ *Evaluation --* ✏️ *Evaluation --* ✏️ *Evaluation*

Student

I think this project was

poor   all right   great

because _____

_____

Student signature _____

Teacher

I think this project was

poor   all right   great

because _____

_____

Teacher signature _____

276

My Project

Date _Nov. 1994_

Student Name _Andy   Grade 1_

Title or Description: _Reading about Dinosaurs_

Completed Sample

Plan of Action:

I want to look at dinosaur pictures and read about dinosaurs. I can read some of the words. My dad will help me with the other words.

If I have time, I'll make a dinosaur out of clay, or wood or something.

Use time from class: _Reading_

✏️ *Evaluation* -- ✏️ *Evaluation* -- ✏️ *Evaluation* -- ✏️ *Evaluation*

Student

I think this project was   poor   all right   (great)

because _I liked reading about dinosaurs._

My clay dinosaur was great!.

Student signature _ANDY_

Teacher

I think this project was   poor   all right   (great)

because _Andy learned a lot in an area that interested him. He learned new skills_

Teacher signature _Ms. Teacher_

PLANNING SHEET for INDIVIDUAL PROJECT

Student name_____ Planning Date _____

This is a description of my proposed project:

_____

_____

_____

_____

_____

_____

_____

_____

_____

_____

Use time from: _____

INSTRUCTOR'S SIGNATURE OF APPROVAL_____ DATE_____

CONCLUSION OF PROJECT

■ Student evaluation   Date_____

This project was (circle one)   EXCELLENT   SATISFACTORY   COULD HAVE BEEN BETTER

Comments:

_____

_____

_____

● Instructor's Evaluation   Date _____

This project was (circle one)   EXCELLENT   SATISFACTORY   COULD HAVE BEEN BETTER

Comments:

_____

_____

_____

PLANNING SHEET for INDIVIDUAL PROJECT

Student name _Katie - grade 1_ Planning Date _3-10-95_

This is a description of my proposed project:

Visit a zoo
I want to see the penguins.
I want to see them jump
into the water.
Mom or Dad will take me
to the zoo.

Completed Sample

Use time from: Reading

INSTRUCTOR'S SIGNATURE OF APPROVAL _Mrs Teacher_ DATE _3-10-95_

CONCLUSION OF PROJECT

Student evaluation Date _3-15-87_

and

This project was (circle one)   (EXCELLENT)   SATISFACTORY   (COULD HAVE BEEN BETTER)

Comments:
I really liked seeing the penguins should have taken
pictures

Instructor's Evaluation Date _4-4-95_

This project was (circle one)   (EXCELLENT)   SATISFACTORY   COULD HAVE BEEN BETTER

Comments:
Good project. Your report to the class was super!

Planning Sheet for Individual Project

Student name _____ Planning Date _____

A. Type of project: (circle one)   report   drama   poster   sketch   flashcards

    other _____

B. Title of Project

_____

_____

C. What the project will look like or be when it is completed (as now "seen" in the mind of the planner). Continue on reverse side if more room is needed.

_____

_____

_____

D. Plan of Procedure (continue on reverse side of page if more room is needed):

_____

_____

_____

_____

_____

Use time from: _____

★ ★ ★ ★ ★ ★ ★ ★ ★ ★ ★ ★ ★ ★ ★

E. This project was not completed because _____
    or
This project was completed and reviewed by _____
                                  (name of person or group)

F. Comments by student completing project: _____

    Project was (circle one):   very satisfying   satisfying   could have been better

G. Comments by teacher/mentor: _____

    Project was (circle one):   excellent   satisfactory   could have been better

_____   _____
Student signature   Date   Teacher/mentor signature   Date

Planning Sheet for Individual Project

Student name ___Jane___   Planning Date __4·12·94__

A. Type of project: (circle one)   report   drama   poster   sketch   flashcards
other ___play___

B. Title of Project
___Harriet Tubman: My Heroine!___   *Completed Sample*

C. What the project will look like or be when it is completed (as now "seen" in the mind of the planner). Continue on reverse side if more room is needed.
___a play that can be performed in our classroom.___

D. Plan of Procedure (continue on reverse side of page if more room is needed):
1. Write the play.
2. Get friends to read it.
3. Make any changes needed.
4. Get friends to act out the play

Use time from: ___spelling___

★ ★ ★ ★ ★ ★ ★ ★ ★ ★ ★ ★ ★ ★

E. This project was not completed because ___project too difficult and I got sick___
or
This project was completed and reviewed by _____
(name of person or group)

F. Comments by student completing project: _____

Project was (circle one):   very satisfying   satisfying   could have been better

G. Comments by teacher/mentor: ___Even if Jane didnt finish she read about Harriet Tubman.___

Project was (circle one):   excellent   satisfactory   could have been better

___Jane___   ___End of School___   ___Mrs. Teacher___   ___End of May___
Student signature   Date   Teacher/mentor signature   Date

My Research Project Plan

Directions: Use this sheet to plan your own research project.

1 QUESTION OR HYPOTHESIS, TOPIC TO BE RESEARCHED:

_____

_____

2 SOURCES OF INFORMATION ON THE TOPIC:

_____

_____

_____

_____

_____

3 METHOD OR PLAN FOR RESEARCHING THE TOPIC:

_____

_____

_____

_____

_____

_____

_____

_____

_____

Student name _____ *Anticipated completion date* _____

Research advisor _____

_____*Project is approved. Approved on this date*_____

_____*Project not approved. The checked* ☑ *need redoing:*

☐ *Question*   ☐ *Sources of information*   ☐ *Method*

Comments:

My Research Project Plan

Directions: Use this sheet to plan your own research project.

1 QUESTION OR HYPOTHESIS, TOPIC TO BE RESEARCHED:

Design an energy-efficient house for south

central Iowa that would be acceptable   *Completed Sample*

to the general public.

2 SOURCES OF INFORMATION ON THE TOPIC:

books and articles on energy efficient

heating and cooling systems

books and charts on standard weather patterns

for south central Iowa - summer & winter

universities within Iowa - talk to people working

in energy efficiency

3 METHOD OR PLAN FOR RESEARCHING THE TOPIC:

1. Design a questionnaire to determine what

persons consider essential/acceptable in a home.

2. Read about energy efficient measures

3. Combine results from questionnaire with

energy efficient information.

If necessary, consult with specialists.

Student name _____   Anticipated completion date _____

Research advisor _____

_____ Project is approved. Approved on *this date*_____

_____ Project not approved. The checked ☑ *need redoing:*

☐ Question   ☐ Sources of information   ☐ Method

Comments:

Student Projects - Ideas & Plans. © Leadership Publishers, 1994

Student Name _____

independent project

My Plan for Independent Project

_____

_____

_____

_____

_____

_____

_____

_____

_____

_____

Expected completion date: _____

Completed project will be reviewed by _____

Project was completed on this date _____

Project was reviewed by: _____

_____

Reviewer's comments:

_____

_____

_____

Student's comments on own project:

_____

_____

_____

_____

_____

Student Name _____Connie_____

My Plan for Independent Project

Write a science fiction story.

Characters: a team of scientists: Professor Jagiot-physicist

    Professor Schmack - biologist

    Professor Johannsen - chemist

Flight crew: Captain Oranz - experienced, daring, irritable,

     likes power

     Radio communications man - Mel Smancy - harbors a secret

     anger towards Captain Oranz.

Conflict-the trip and medical expedition goes fine. On return trip to

Earth, Mel refuses to send radio communications. They could be lost.

Expected completion date: ___2 weeks - April 6, 1994___

Completed project will be reviewed by ___classmates and/or teacher___

••

Project was completed on this date ___April 15,___ 1994

Project was reviewed by: ___classmates and teacher___

Completed Sample

Reviewer's comments:

Classmates- neat story. Question, "How come Mel waited so long

  before he got even with Captain Oranz?"

Teacher: good plot, strong beginning and ending, story moves right

Student's comments on own project: along. Strong conflict.

"This was my first science fiction story. I like it but I

don't want to write any more science fiction. I think I'll

follow the adventures of Captain Oranz and Mel here on Earth."

independent project

This certificate is issued

to

_____

for

_____

_____   _____
Instructor   Date

EXCELLENT ACHIEVEMENT AWARD

Issued to _____
For This Achievement:

_____

_____

_____

_____

Date:_____   Issued by:

Topical Index
Topic/Page(s)   * profiles a student project.

* profiles a student project